Complete Guide to Knitting & Crochet

Nicki Trench

A useful guide to knitting & crochet – featuring simple & fun projects

Parragon

Bath · New York · Singapore · Hong Kong · Cologne · Delhi · Melbourne

This edition published in 2007

Parragon
Queen Street House
4 Queen Street
Bath BA1 1HE, UK

ISBN 978-1-4054-8610-1

The author would like to thank the following people:
Pattern designers: Vikki Haffenden, Jane Rota, Nicki Trench, Sian Brown, Annalisa Dunne, Joey Griffiths, Beryl Oakes, Amy Phipps, Zara Pool, Nikki Ryan, Rebecca Smith and Emmaline Woodman
Models: Camilla Perkins, Rebecca Hawes, Tom Sheffield, Roxy Walton
Stylist: Vikki Haffenden, Sue Lee
Assistant Stylist: Hannah Jenkinson

For Butler and Tanner:
Project editor: Julian Flanders
Editor: Emma Clegg
Designer: Carole McDonald
Pattern checker: Margaret O'Mara

Location and techniques photography: Carole McDonald
Studio photography: Don Last
Art works: Sue Lee

Additional photo s provided by:
Knitting: Corbis UK page 12, Debbie Bliss pages 14 & 15, Getty images page 11, Rex Features page 15, Rowan Yarns pages 3, 14 & 15
Crochet: Rowan Yarns page 102, page 132 left: Piku of England, middle: Colinette Yarns, right: Mary-Helen

Printed in China

Contents-Knitting

	Introduction	6
PART ONE	Knitting then... and now	10
PART TWO	What you need... and what to do with it	20
PART THREE	Patterns... funky fashions	52
	The easy jumper	56
	Unisex hoody	58
	Alpaca cardigan	62
	Fingerless gloves	66
	Poncho	68
	Cotton summer hat	70
	Dare-to-wear bikini	72
	Mobile phone/iPod cover	74
	Leg warmers	76
	Throw	77
	Tasseled garter stitch scarf and Garter stitch scarf	78
	Fluffy silky-chic scarf	80
	Beanie hat	81
	Beaded make-up bag	82
	Funky cushions	84
	Button handbag	86
	Dog jackets	87
	Rose top	90
	Yarn tote bag	94
	Needle udder	96
PART FOUR		
	20 mistakes that every knitter should make	98
	Stockists	99

Contents- Crochet

PART ONE   New-Age Crochet   100

PART TWO   What you need... and what to do with it   106

PART THREE   Patterns... to get you hooked   136

    Beanie hat   140
    Flower blanket   142
    Frill shawl   144
    Pet's playmat   146
    Summer flower camisole   148
    Stripy dog blanket   150
    Striped hairbands   152
    Mesh bag   154
    Tie bolero   157
    Flower-power beaded belt   162
    Summer brimmed hat   164
    Daisy cashmere scarf   167
    Fingerless gloves   170
    Beaded purse   172
    Ribbon slippers   174
    Hot-water bottle cover   176
    Cushion cake   178
    Loopy cushion   181
    Clutch bag with bow   184
    Placemat and coaster   186

PART FOUR

    Love questionnaire   188
    Stockists and useful addresses   189
    Index   190-192

Introduction

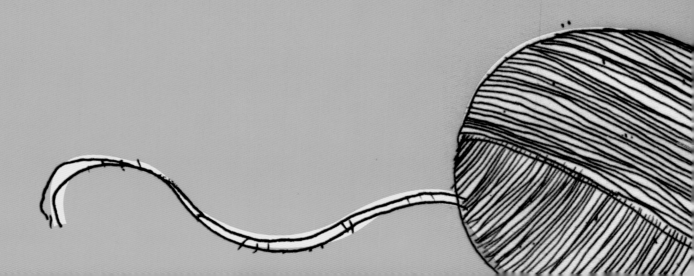

This is a book about modern knitting and crochet. Even five years ago mentioning the words 'modern', 'knitting' and 'crochet' all in the same sentence would have seemed extraordinary and unbelievable. There are several reasons for this.

Catwalk designers such as Alexander McQueen, Donna Karan and Stella McCartney consistently have hand knits or crochet in their collections. High street fashion shops have been quick to follow this trend with the result that most people now have some sort of fashion knitting or crochet in their wardrobe. Trimmings and fashion accessories make a knitted or crocheted item much more interesting than traditional knitwear designs and the use of ribbon, beads and cute bows appeal to both old and young. From slinky pieces using fine yarns or chunky chic using newly developed superchunky yarns, hand crafted fashion is here to stay.

Women have been struggling for years to take their stand in the workplace and are now feeling confident without the need to express themselves in male terms by wearing padded shoulders and suits as a form of armour-plating. They are finding a voice of their own and realise they can be just as effective in the workplace in a feminine, soft, luxurious hand knitted garment and be taken just as seriously. After toiling all day in the office, women are keen to take up an unashamedly girly hobby such as knitting and crochet and are keen to replicate designer garments with their own pair of knitting needles or crochet hooks.

This is backed up by the surge of interest in the general craft industry. Craft Hobby & Stitch International, Europe's largest trade event for the art, craft, needlecraft and hobby industry, welcomed a record number of visitors to its recent show.

More than 7,250 buyers attended, an increase of 5 per cent on the previous year's attendance. The number of exhibitors from the yarn industry had increased considerably, which reflects the growing interest in this creative and practical craft.

Knitting is the new rock 'n' roll

At a recent craft fair run by Country Living magazine in the UK, Laughinghens.com, a popular online wool store, opened a stall selling knitting and crochet products. The buzz round the corridors of the fair was, 'I hear knitting is the new rock 'n' roll', and gasps of delight were audible as visitors turned the corner to see a stall full of beautiful colour, a whole range of textures and a host of many easily-achievable projects such

as bunting, cushions, pretty knitted bags and glamorous crocheted throws/afghans. It appears that today's knitters are rediscovering the addiction that our grandmothers have passed on.

Women have discovered that knitting and crochet can be for pleasure rather than necessity. It follows trends in home cooking, gardening and DIY. So whether cooking with fresh veg from our garden or knitting our own clothes – they're more enjoyable now that the stress of survival has been removed from them and our modern lives.

The Craft Yarn Council of America says more than 20 million men and women are knitting and crocheting in the USA. Knit café's are springing up throughout the US. The latest is Knit New York, a very cool place to eat pastries, drink lattes and knit with cool, luscious yarns. They run regular classes on knitting and crochet and are encouraging the new trend for men by running men–only classes. This popularity in knitting and crochet is filtering across the Atlantic to the UK and cities and towns throughout the UK and the USA are holding knit events. Vikki Haffenden, who has organised the Brighton Big Knit In for the last couple of years says, 'it's a pleasure to see knitters of all ages sharing their skills and encouraging new participants in this ancient craft'. Knitting and crochet workshop places are often booked up well in advance and the shops that are encouraging the young and offer a trendy lifestyle image are often proving to be incredibly successful.

Colleges both in the US and UK have been inundated with applications from students wanting to learn how to knit and crochet. Demand for evening classes as well as for graduate places on textile courses is increasing as the young are catching on to this new craze. Thankfully, with all this demand, there are still some grandmothers out there able to teach this ancient skill.

In the UK three new magazines have emerged to catch on to demand for more information about yarn and knitting/crochet products: Knitting, Simply Knitting and Knit Today. In the USA magazines such as Vogue Knitting continue to produce high-quality patterns and news for knitters and crocheters.

More than great pastimes

But there may be more to knitting and crochet than simply being great pastimes. A research project taking place at Cardiff University Psychology Department is looking into the theory that knitting and crochet are highly effective tools for dealing with the complexities of stress, pain, depression and long-term illness, and also for being a very useful aid to those trying to give up smoking or losing weight.

Betsan Corkhill, who owns and run Stitchlinks, a member-based friendship network that combines the therapeutic benefits of knitting, crochet and cross stitching with practical health information, says, 'Anecdotal evidence is strong that knitting and crochet are powerful tools to manage a range of illnesses. They can change behaviour and attitudes, calm panic and anxiety and distract from pain and depression. They may even be changing the brain itself'.

Tales of the extraordinary health benefits of knitting and crochet continue to grow. Many US schools are so convinced of its use in aiding concentration in children that they are encouraging children to knit during class. 'The general perception is that if a kid is knitting, they're not paying attention, but they are listening,' says Devorah Zamansky, the assistant principal at the Manhattan Centre of Science and Mathematics, where pupils are allowed to knit and crochet while attending lessons.

So what can you say about an activity that makes you healthy, happy and with a satisfying result without the need for treadmills, supplements, surgery, postgraduate degrees or a bank loan? What you say is, 'Where do I start?' And the answer is, 'Right here'.

PART ONE

Knitting then...

... and now

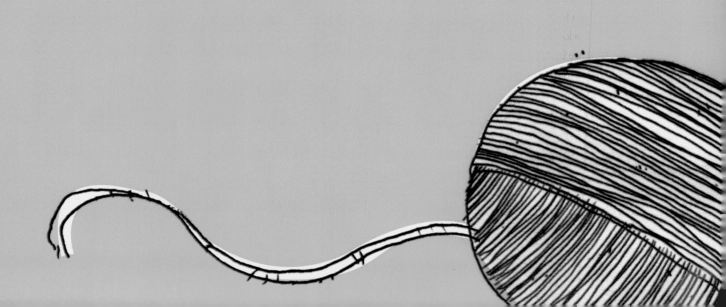

Why Has Knitting Come Back Into Fashion?

The simple answer is that such an addictive pastime can't just disappear without making a comeback. Knitting is given a new lease of life as it is rediscovered by each new generation. Recently knitting's stock has soared because modern couturiers have for several seasons presented beautifully designed knitwear with a hefty price tag and it's not hard to see that these same designs can be made at home for a fraction of the price. And, besides, what other activity can turn the making of something into a party?

Ancient purls of wisdom

Knitters rule – and there is no doubt about it. Was there a time when we didn't knit? Well, there must have been. The earliest traces of knitting as we know it are cotton socks and other knitted fragments dating from AD 1200–1500 in Islamic Egypt, although anklet socks with a stocking-stitch-type construction have also been found in Egypt dating from as early as the third century. So there's an important lesson: if your civilisation is in final decline, always keep your feet warm.

The Britons kept sheep and wove wool long before the Roman invasion, and the establishment by the Romans of a factory at Winchester improved their methods. Knitting came into the European picture in the 5th century, when the Moors from North Africa invaded Spain.

By the 13th century England was the greatest wool-producing country in Europe. Knitting was the principal method of making socks and women's stockings. Hosiery, the name still used to describe these products, is derived from the old English word 'hose', which means 'a covering for the leg'. Gradually knitting came to be used to make more elaborate garments such as jumpers and jackets and other items of fitted clothing. Although this does depend on your definition of 'elaborate' – if you've ever turned a heel on a sock you'll know that this is no rudimentary process.

The image of women knitting 'while the guillotine falls' during the French Revolution is striking, but it owes more to Charles Dickens's novel A Tale of Two Cities than it does to any historical fact.

Knitting wasn't always considered the occupation of women. Indeed, some historians think that men invented the craft, probably fishermen developing a technique for making fishing nets. The knitted craft remains closely allied with the fishing trade, with fishermen still wearing Ganseys, or traditional fishermens' sweaters, so densely knitted in worsted yarn that they are almost windproof and waterproof. Individual knitted designs were often used for the various fishing village communities. In the marshy Les Landes area in southwest France, the medieval peasants kept huge herds of sheep. The shepherds would walk around on stilts so that they could take longer steps, cover more ground and see further. They used to knit while they walked using a knitting belt to keep their wool safe. They were vegetarian and used the sheep for their manure rather than meat, so they didn't kill them. They knitted their own gaiters to keep their feet warm and felted their own jackets from the fleeces of their sheep.

Women do their bit for the war effort knitting socks from recycled wool circa 1940.

Knitting for victory

In the 20th century women were urged to knit for the troops in the two world wars, especially the First World War when the men faced severe shortages of socks, vests and washcloths. In this conflict, the image of the resolute soldier shivering in a trench was implanted in the minds of the world's womenfolk. In the 1939–45 war, millions of knitted pieces were produced. Posters produced by organisations such as the American Red Cross in 1943 urged womenfolk to keep knitting: 'Our boys need SOX, knit your bit'. It was a real act of love, and even the British lads of the Eighth Army, sweltering in the Western Desert, could not help but be moved upon receipt of a lovingly hand-knitted item from home. There was even a free Red Cross kit featuring the hand-dyed yarn, a pattern and the double-pointed and finishing needles necessary to make a pair of military socks. During this period, knitting was even being featured on the front of *Life* magazine in the USA.

Fashion revolution

In the 1950s and 1960s, colour in knitting arrived with a bang. After the drabness of the war, colour and motif knitting became the new knitting fads. Girls were taught to knit in schools, where it was still regarded as a necessity and a useful skill. The knitted 'twin-set', comprising a cardigan over a matching short-sleeved top, came into fashion. It made another brief comeback in the 1970s and will almost inevitably surface again in future decades.

Did knitting ever really go away?

Frankly, yes. The 1970s and 1980s were a particularly brutal time for knitting. Girls, not wanting to look like their grannies, turned their backs on knitting and immersed themselves in glam rock. The increased availability of low-cost machine-knitted items made knitting an expensive luxury, when you could buy a jumper off the peg cheaper than it could be knitted. It was the start of the convenience culture, with equivalent cultural parallels being plasterboard, Artex, fish fingers and instant potato.

There was an abundance of cheap clothing made in artificial fibres, with the novelty of chucking everything in

During the 1940s and 1950s knitting was tasteful and high fashion…

the automatic washing machine being much too hard to resist. Wool started to be replaced by acrylic yarn. As wool shops were interested only in selling manmade fibres, the pure natural brands were pushed aside to make way for the vibrant colours and wacky styles of the era. Rather than being appreciated for its beauty, wool was instead associated with heavy and itchy knits. And with a washing machine in every kitchen, who was going to mess around with that woollen material that shrank and clumped up as soon as it went anywhere near water?

The craft industry in general went into decline as women rose to the challenge of being equal players in the workplace. Women either embraced capitalism and adopted big hair and big shoulders, or put on a boiler suit and picketed bus garages as part of the feminist 'Reclaim the Night' campaign. Knitting was what you didn't do – it had become a symbol of passivity and staying at home. Whether you dressed to the political left or right, staying in just wasn't an option.

Knitting was no longer being taught in schools and was slowly being relegated to the confines of 'hippy' culture, in a time before hippy was hip. Knitters began to develop a reputation for being part of the macrobiotic, faddy set and nobody with a Filofax would be seen dead with knitting needles or a crochet hook at this time.

... even in Hollywood.

But the 1960s and 1970s were barren, knitting was unfashionable and downright bad taste.

Knitting Bites Back

Knitting is now making a comeback and defying the idea that it cannot form an enriching part of a modern woman's life. Women now realise that they can juggle different aspects of themselves, so can, if they choose, be mothers and craftswomen, have serious careers and still go clubbing on a Saturday night. The knitting industry has been quick to recognise this. In an effort to modernise the reputation of knitting, companies such as Vogue and Rowan have produced knitting pattern books rather than leaflets, and their quality photography now shows knitting to be at the height of fashion, bearing no resemblance to the old images of dull men in balaclavas and grimacing children sporting itchy swimwear. Of course, you can also buy high-quality knitwear, but when the idea of an acquired skill comes into play, the cost ceases to be the point.

As well as stylish patterns, the yarn itself has taken on a new life. The old acrylic fibres used to build you up with static electricity, but now top-quality, natural wools are mixed with a small amount of manmade fibres, restoring the tradition of natural wools while at the same time benefiting from modern-day developments. The easy-care results are another bonus that has drawn people back to knitting.

The cult of the accessory

The TV schedule is full of home-improvement programmes and knitting has also moved in this direction, becoming a source of home-decoration ideas and accessories. Instead of knitting only jumpers and complicated cardigans, knitters can now bring individuality and creativeness into their home by making items such as cushion covers and throws. You're not just knitting now – you're following a lifestyle pattern.

Yarn producers have tried to encourage knitters back to the craft by producing speciality yarn. The sumptuous mixes of yarn, such as Merino wool, Cashmere and Alpaca, are hard to resist. The colours have also been brought up to date with historical heritage palettes that tone in with the speciality paints in our modern interiors. All the perceived advantages of using pure manmade fibres have therefore vanished. People are knitting with fabrics other than wool: there is ribbon yarn, chenille, eyelash yarn and hand-dyed slubs, along with the superchunky yarn that knits up on giant-size needles, meaning that knitting is no longer a time-intensive pastime. If weather forecasts predict snow tomorrow, you can whip up several superchunky hats in a single evening.

21st-century knitting

Knitwear is in fashion – just pick up a copy of any fashion magazine and you will see hand-knitted scarves, jumpers and skirts in the new textures and superchunky styles.

As a result, further-education textile courses have a new influx of students enrolling for knitting. The knitters of today regard what they do as a branch of art and in their minds they are a world away from the familiar image of granny knitting for her grandchildren. There is no need, however,

to ignore those knitters who've kept the craft alive through the years; grandmas are now hailed as new gurus by the young knitters of today.

Celebrity knitting – the new yoga

There are often articles in the local and national press with a knitting story. Knitting seems now to have caught the eye of the media, particularly when a hot celebrity gets out his or her needles. Knitting is now hailed as the 'new yoga' as celebrities, young professionals and yarn enthusiasts from all walks of life are getting down to knitting. Geri Halliwell, Julia Roberts, Catherine Zeta-Jones, Russell Crowe, Kate Moss, Sarah Jessica Parker, Daryl Hannah, Uma Thurman, Julianne Moore, Courtney Cox-Arquette and Madonna are all knitting on and off set – it's obviously an ideal pastime between takes and the passion of these stars is influencing the proliferation of new knitters all over the world.

Psychological warmth

And is it any wonder? Knitting is a wonderful retreat from an increasingly tough world. It's calming, primeval, just like dancing to a plain drumbeat – in, round, through and off. The soft touch of the yarn is comforting, a pleasant contrast to the harshness of the computer keyboard and our new culture of tough words such as hard drive, megabyte, metatag and USB. The restorative powers of knitting demonstrate the calming effect of repetition. As you knit,

your breathing adjusts to its rhythm and the whole process becomes a soothing and meditative experience.

The effect on your mind is similar to distance running or saying a rosary – it puts you within reach of a higher awareness. Your mind begins to behave in the same way as your brain works just before you go to sleep – relaxed, but at the same time aware – and enters what is called 'a suggestible state'. If you put on language learning tapes while you're knitting, you'll be truly amazed at your progress. Or try listening to baroque music as you knit – Bach, Vivaldi, Corelli and Pachelbel are all big hitters in the world of baroque 'n' roll. Bach, especially, gives you a day ticket to nirvana.

Socks and the City: Sarah Jessica Parker and Kristin Davis chatting, smiling, and, of course, knitting on set, winter 2001.

There's a real zen to knitting – and it makes you realise that the zen is in the task itself. On a recent knit night, as the stitch count grew higher, I began a conversation with the woman next to me. We were so intent on the job in hand that we didn't make eye contact, normally regarded as essential for effective communication, during the whole conversation. No, on we went talking about real issues and exchanging considered views. It felt comforting at the time, however astonishing in retrospect.

Rock 'n' roll or knit 'n' purl?

But the real hardcore of knitters are being hailed as guerrilla knitters. They have taken up the craft as a new cause, promoting knitting as a hip and cool hobby that should be taken very seriously. One such group is Cast Off, formed in 2000 and based in London. Its members' aims are to encourage the art of knitting and urge people to pick up their needles wherever they are – in pubs, nightclubs or on the Tube. They have organised knit-in parties on the Circle Line of the London Underground where knitters pop on at their stop in a chosen carriage, knit away for a few circles around London and get off when they've finished. Cast Off has also organised a knitting event at London's Victoria & Albert Museum that an amazing 4,000 people attended. The atmosphere was steamy with participants knitting and purling to the rhythms of rock. There was a DJ, beer, and someone in a pink knitted Elvis wig, people were dancing with their knitting, and everyone who came in was offered free needles and yarn. More amazing still, there was an even mix of women and men – this was definitely not knitting as our grandmothers knew it. Cast Off also holds 'knit-ins' at summer festivals. There are other similar groups emerging around the UK.

Inspired by the book *Stitch 'n Bitch* by Debbie Stoller, Stitch 'n Bitch groups in the USA have really taken off. There are knitting-group meetings in every state, with people from all walks of life getting together at cafés, bars and community centres to work on projects, help each other with their knitting projects and chat. According to the Craft Yarn Council of America, the number of knitters under 35 grew by more than 400 per cent between 1998 and 2000.

It seems that knitting circles in the USA are following the example set by book clubs in providing fun, companionship and community. There is a big knitting community at Yale, where there is a whole scene of women very serious about their handiwork; one student even knitted her way through her maths classes one semester and later married her maths tutor. A couple of male students turned up at the Yale Stitch 'n Bitch classes, only to be turned away for very obviously being attracted to the classes for the girls not the needles. Men interested in knitting, however, are warmly welcomed.

The internet has undoubtedly had a huge influence on the rise of knitters in the 21st century. The buying of knitting products has soared with the emergence of websites selling yarn and patterns via mail order, while knitting-forum chat rooms help knitters keep in touch and bring together the knitting community. So knitting has now emerged well and truly as a cool hobby – increasing numbers of people are discovering that the rhythmic clacking of the needles and comforting feel of the yarn let the demands of 21st-century pressures slip away and off the needle.

Extreme Knitting

Knitters are getting so obsessed with their knitting that they can't put it down. So forget extreme ironing and take up extreme knitting.

Knit Groups

> They say that staying in is the new going out, and what is better than staying in with friends doing something you enjoy? And a few casual drinks aren't going to be a cause of stress. It might mean you lose a few stitches, but nobody is going to breathalyse you while knitting under the influence.

Why knit groups?

Knit groups started when women used to knit for pin money in the evenings. They would go to each other's houses to save on candles and heat and, without doubt, to chat. Nothing beats hanging out with like-minded people who have a shared intent. Men watch football and talk about sport whereas women knit and talk about life, the universe and everything. If you have the choice between joining a knit night or a book club, which would you choose? Sure, the book club is a great idea and it means you'll have a real intellectual challenge, but it's still consuming rather than producing, and you may find that really great books are ignored by the club in favour of the works of a no-hope literary-prize wannabe.

Knitting is productive, cheap and safe, but most of all it is therapeutic. As our society becomes increasingly impersonal, a group that provides mutual support and fun, is cheaper than many other evening activities and offers more effective results is very appealing. Once you start knitting you'll find that you start communicating with your fellow knitters, sometimes pouring out your emotions and you can end up disclosing all your secrets. Knitting is also an excellent way of giving up smoking, as your hands are kept busy and, in any case, you might set fire to your yarn. Its cheaper than psychotherapy and who wants to sit on a couch with nothing to do.

Professional women find themselves thrust into a tough and competitive male world and this can take its toll. Knitting is an ideal opportunity to get out of the go-get drive, switch off and do the girly bonding thing, offering a chill-out for women who are frantically trying to do it all. Knitting tends to appeal to creative people and women who are not afraid of being girly. 'Knit night' groups are being organised in public knitting venues as well as private houses. A screening of *Bridget Jones's Diary* took place in London exclusively for a London-based knitting group. Groups of knitters are sprouting up everywhere in the UK, the USA and Europe. Meetings are being held for relaxation and for the pursuit of art. While some women choose to adopt feminism, social climbing and sexual equality, others adopt creative crafts.

For whatever reason, most just like to meet for fun, to drink tea, hot chocolate or wine and eat cake. Most knitters are female, but there are a growing number of men joining the knit groups. The members are principally in their 20s and 30s, but they are also drawn from a wide range of ages. The cult is so established that there are now knitting and surfing holidays being organised on the coast and you can even, if you choose, combine knitting and parachuting.

Knitting promotes communication and helps produce a positive and productive attitude to life.

Knitting and Dating

Follow these rules and your purls may get you a diamond

RULE 1

Do not knit your boyfriend a jumper until you are well and truly into your relationship (at least 10 years)

There is a well-known superstition that if you knit your boyfriend a jumper you will, within a week, be on your own. Much of the abandoned, unfinished knitting in the loft can be attributed to lost boyfriends. If you start knitting him a jumper, it is probably only at the point of shaping the left-hand shoulder that he leaves you for the blonde up the road.

RULE 2

Do not wear itchy fabrics on your first date.

Instead, choose something silky with a satin feel. Snuggle up in something cashmere or silk – mohair or eyelash yarn might get up his nose and he may think he has an allergy to you.

RULE 3

Don't take your knitting on your first date.

As difficult as it is to put down or finish that row, leave it at home. Guys will want to feel that the attention is on them, not on your knitting.

RULE 4

Do take your knitting on your first date.

This applies only if it's a speed-dating event – this is a great opportunity to knit because if the guy you're talking to is boring, at least you can make use of the time. And if you can't find anything interesting to say, you can talk about what you're knitting.

RULE 5

Don't let dating interfere with your knitting.

Get on his good side by suggesting you both stay in and watch the football. He'll be amazed and think he's hit the jackpot – a girl who likes football! Just snuggle up next to him and whip out your knitting while he's cheering on his favourite team. Bingo, you're both happy.

RULE 6

Invest in a hands-free telephone headset.

Then you can carry on knitting when he calls you on the phone. This also helps eliminate all the 'you hang up, no, you hang up' banter.

RULE 7

Make sure your needles are safely stowed away before those tender sofa moments.

You could be just at that critical moment and your 7mm needles may give him a nasty surprise.

'*Knit your hearts out with unslipping knot*'

William Shakespeare, Anthony and Cleopatra

What do we do in a knit group?

Well, we knit and we talk… mmmmm… that's just about it.
Communicating is one thing that women have a natural
facility for. We support our friends, share knowledge and help
each other. Fellow knitters are reassuring and supportive of
each other's knitting and there is rarely any competitive
element. We discuss current affairs, problems, health, family
and work; we giggle and laugh; and sometimes we just sit in
silence with the sound of our needles busying away. Silent
pauses are respected, someone may be counting their stitches.

Setting up a knit group

All you need is some knitting and a good supply of soft
drinks, and wine for those knitting less complicated items
who don't need to keep a crystal-clear head. Once you're
brave enough to tell people that you're setting up a knit
group, you'll be surprised at the number of people who will
remember their half-finished knitting in the loft. They'll say
it in an embarrassed and shifty way at first and then the
passion will pour out with descriptions of the texture and
colour of the yarn as it slips through their fingers and slides
off the needles. The touch and feel of the cold aluminium or
the warm bamboo needles will entice such alerted minds…
and then you'll find they'll be begging to come.

Monday nights are best. You're rarely hampered by other
commitments and you can catch up on any gossip after the
weekend in a relaxed, unthreatening atmosphere – 7.30 p.m.
to 10.00 p.m. is perfect, allowing you to get home at a
reasonable time. You can alternate between friends' houses.
Or if you have a really comfortable venue such as a friendly
pub with a supportive landlord, that's perfect. But pick your
pub carefully; one knit group was recently chucked out of a
pub on a Monday night. Make sure you buy a few gin and
tonics during the evening and don't stand in front of the TV
when the football's on. Remember, you need comfy sofas and
chairs and a clean floor for your wool when it rolls out of
your bag.

When people see you knitting in public, they can't resist
coming over and talking to you about what you're making,
especially if you're using the new funky yarn that is now
so popular.

Bristol knitting group

PART TWO

What you need...

... and what to do with it

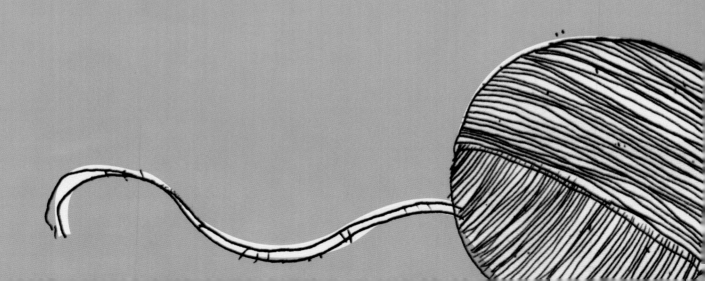

Yarn

New types of yarns are partly responsible for knitting making such a comeback. Some are so beautiful that you just want to have that sumptuous ball of wool next to you on the sofa without a knitting needle in sight.

There are so many variations of yarn you can buy, in so many different textures and colours, that it's hard to know where to start. If you start from a pattern, then use the pattern to focus your choice of yarn and any other choices that need to be made. Or you might first discover a yarn that you just can't resist and choose a pattern afterwards.

WHERE TO BUY YARN

Department stores

These are generally a good source of yarn, although their supplies can be limited.

High-street wool shops

These more traditional specialist shops are now quite thin on the ground. This is generally because of a lack of demand for the often uninspiring types of yarn they used to sell. However, new specialist shops are now slowly emerging that are catering for the modern taste for natural and varied yarn.

Internet companies

The internet is probably going to be your best starting point. Internet companies have been quick to meet the growing demand for knitting yarn so you can now browse your laptop in comfort and have the yarn delivered right to your door. And what a pleasure when you receive your parcel full of knitting goodies – it's just like receiving a present in the post! Find an internet company that is willing to give you advice, too. The local wool shop used to provide guidance on patterns, yarn and knitting equipment and any internet company selling yarn should fulfil the same role for you.

Charity shops

Pop into any charity shop to have a look around as they can sometimes prove a good source of yarn. Obviously, there are no guarantees, but if you rummage around enough you may find something really marvellous. Remember that it will be even more important to knit a tension square if there are no labels on the yarn.

eBay

This auction site has a selection of yarn for web auction. While you can't always find an exact yarn or quantity, it's a good place for finding discount yarn.

YARN TYPES

Here is a list of yarn types that will help you unravel the vocabulary of knitting.

Wool

Wool comes from many different types of sheep, some with much softer wool than others. The fleece from the Spanish-bred Merino sheep has become popular in recent years – it's very fine and soft and available from most manufacturers. Other fine wools include Delaine Merino, Shetland and Debouillet. Apparently there is a fine wool that comes from the North Ronaldsay sheep, which lives wild on this Orkney island and grazes not on grass but on seaweed – and it is this that makes its underbelly fleece incredibly soft. The wool is hard to source, and it can take several days to reach the island depending on the weather. Medium wools include Dorset, Suffolk, Shropshire and Navajo Churro; long wools include Lincoln, Cotswold, Teeswater and Shetland; and coarse wools include Swaledale, Black Welsh Mountain and

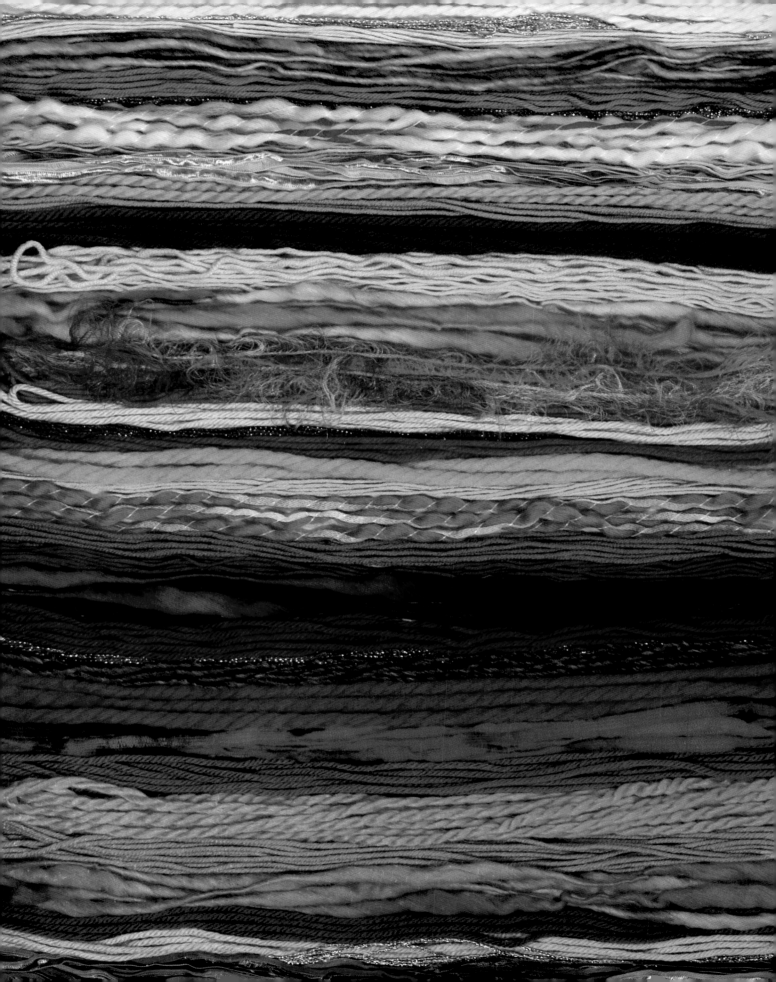

Cheviot. Some wool from Iceland and South America can be very rough and you may find bits of wood and straw tangled up in it. Not so perfect against your body, therefore, but good for chunky cardigans and those people who can stand the discomfort of a Tibetan hat.

Silk

Silk yarn is an expensive investment, but before you turn to a more economical hobby, just have a careful look at some. Silk creates a light and luxurious yarn that makes lovely summer tops or wraps when knitted. It can stretch, but it feels incredibly self-indulgent to the touch – and using silk yarn does give you great knitting caché.

Cotton

This yarn is light and absorbent. It is not as stretchy as wool, but you can buy a wool/cotton mix that works well. Because of its lightness, it is good for a knitted summer garment.

Other natural yarns

Yarns from animals other than sheep, namely the Angora goat (Mohair), the Alpaca (Alpaca), goats or rabbits (Angora) or the underbelly of a goat (Cashmere) are becoming hugely popular. They are very warm and comfortingly soft, the type of yarn that you want to pick up and hold to your face, cooing that you must knit something with it. These types of yarn sometimes come in a wool or silk mix.

Acrylic

This is easy to wash and inexpensive. It is not as warm as natural fibres, however, and the colours look less appealing. This yarn was one of the reasons why knitting went out of fashion in the 1970s and 1980s. Don't look at me, it's not my favourite. But it has some uses, and sometimes a blend of acrylic and wool fibres works well enough.

Ribbon yarn

Usually a manmade fibre (most often polyester), this yarn comes in a whole range of beautiful colours and textures. This fabric yarn is fantastic for knitting because it knits up well. If you are knitting a garment, try to find a yarn that has a bit of stretch in it.

Eyelash yarn

This fine and hairy yarn is usually made of polyester and is very soft and non-itchy, despite having the appearance of something off a dog's back. I wouldn't recommend knitting a whole jumper out of it unless you want to look like a yeti, but it's great for cuffs, collars and accessories. It could be used to make a really funky bag or scarf (see page 80). Eyelash yarn is available in some truly wacky colours.

PLY

Knitting yarn is available in the following thicknesses, each one suitable for a different type of knitting.

4 ply

This thin yarn is used for making light garments, such as summer tops or baby clothes.

Double knitting (dk)

Still a fine wool, this is commonly used for fine garments and baby clothes.

Aran or Worsted

A versatile ply and the most common, this is about twice as thick as double knitting. Good for beginners.

Chunky

This is about twice as thick as Aran or worsted. It knits on larger needles and is good for jumpers, hats, scarves and gloves.

Superchunky

This yarn is increasingly becoming the most popular and is largely responsible for the recent revival of interest in knitting. When knitted up into jumpers and scarves, it makes a real fashion statement. It is knitted on supersize needles, usually 15mm or 20mm, so you can knit a hat or a scarf in one evening. It is perfect for knitters who have other things to do as well as knit.

Hanks, skeins and balls

Yarn is sold by weight and length. It is usually sold in 25g, 50g or 100g weights and the length varies according to the thickness and gauge of the yarn. The length and the weight should be given on the label.

In most shops yarn will come in a wound ball, but sometimes it will come in a hank or a skein. This is a big coil of yarn wrapped in a twist to save it from coming loose. Yarn hanks are what memories are made of. Nearly all yarn used to be packaged like this and my early memories of knitting are of holding up my aching arms for my grandmother so she could wind it into a ball. Either find someone to hold up their two arms for you (the preferable option) or, in the absence of a willing participant, push a couple of chairs together the distance of the size of the hanks, put the hank around the chairs and wind. I find that people love holding up their arms for ball winding. It's at times like this that you'll feel blessed to have a partner who's a keen and boastful fishing enthusiast ('It was *this* big!').

Reading a yarn label

There's a great deal of information on these labels and they are very useful, although the print is often small so a magnifying glass may be required. You will find the brand name, the yarn name and its knitting weight (for example dk or double knit). The label will also tell you what the yarn is made of and the length and weight of the yarn in the ball. There will be a diagram of the recommended knitting gauge, washing and pressing instructions and the recommended needle size. It will also have the yarn's shade number and the dye lot.

Don't throw the label away until you are absolutely sure you have finished with it. If you run out of yarn in the middle of knitting that last sleeve, you might need to find the same dye lot, so you will need the label to check the number when getting back to your yarn supplier. Yarn is dyed in batches (lots) and these dye lots can vary slightly, so it's always best to try to match them up if you can.

Equipment

Here is a list of the equipment and accessories that are either essential or useful to knitters.

NEEDLES

Well, how can you knit without them? Knitting needles come in several sizes. They have developed significantly since our foremothers' day, with the points getting pointier and the bamboo getting smoother.

I've seen people use knitting needles for all sorts of activities: testing to see if a cake is cooked, scratching backs, mini javelin (soon to be an Olympic sport), drumming, picking teeth and playing Ker-Plunk! My mother was even stabbed in the leg by one and still proudly shows her scar:

apparently there's nothing like a scrap in a Gateshead bingo parlour to bring out the swordswoman in us all.

Needle measurements

Just to confuse you, there are three measurements used in knitting patterns: UK, US and metric. To confuse you even more, in the UK we no longer use the UK measurement, but the metric measurement.

Needle width

The grey needles in the thinner sizes are generally made from aluminium; as they get thicker they are made from plastic. Needle width, or the diameter of the needle, is crucial. Thick needles are usually used with thick yarn and thin needles with thin yarn. All good patterns and yarn labels will give the recommended needle size for the yarn and pattern. But, depending on the tension you wish to create in the piece, you may end up knitting with a needle size that's bigger or smaller than recommended.

Bamboo needles are becoming very popular – they have a warm feel and are more natural. It's worth investing in good-quality bamboo, as the cheaper versions tend to snag the yarn and split.

If you scour charity shops you can find all sorts of yummy needles. The needle measurement may be in old sizes, so make sure you check with a needle conversion table. I've recently seen tortoiseshell needles for sale on eBay and I've known glass needles to have been found at a charity shop, so keep your eyes peeled. Remember, however, that new needles have a much pointier design and are therefore easier to knit with.

Circular needles

Circular needles have two pointy ends, shorter than normal straight needles, and a plastic length in the middle of varying sizes. They are usually used to knit in the round, particularly items such as socks or hats. Many knitters, however, also use them to knit flat work. If you are knitting something that takes lots of stitches, such as a throw, a circular needle is excellent. Make sure you choose the right length circular needle, one with a long enough centrepiece to hold the stitches. Knitters are increasingly taking to circular needles as they are so portable. They have been highly recommended in the USA as the perfect needles to take to music festivals; the short needles don't poke too far out of your bag and the knitting and needle is in one piece so you are less likely to lose your needles and ruin any valuable knitting time while away from home.

Double-pointed needles

These are just what they say – they have a point at either end of the needle. They are shorter than standard needles and usually come in packs of four or five. They are often used for knitting socks. This process is not as intimidating as it looks –

just keep knitting until you get to the next needle point. As you work you are prompted by the needles and the working sequence becomes obvious.

Cable needles

Cable needles are used to hold your stitches with knitting cables. They usually come in either large or small sizes.

TAPE MEASURE

Use a cloth tape rather than the inflexible metal ones you get in a toolbox – otherwise you might end up knitting a girder. In the old days there was always a measurement drawn on the side of patterns, but as most patterns are in magazines or books now, you need to carry your own.

SCISSORS

The most oft-heard cry at knit nights after 'Where did you put that other bottle of wine?' is 'Who's got the scissors?' It's always best to carry your own and I would suggest tying them to your knitting bag so that nobody can nick them. Medium-sized sharp ones are the best.

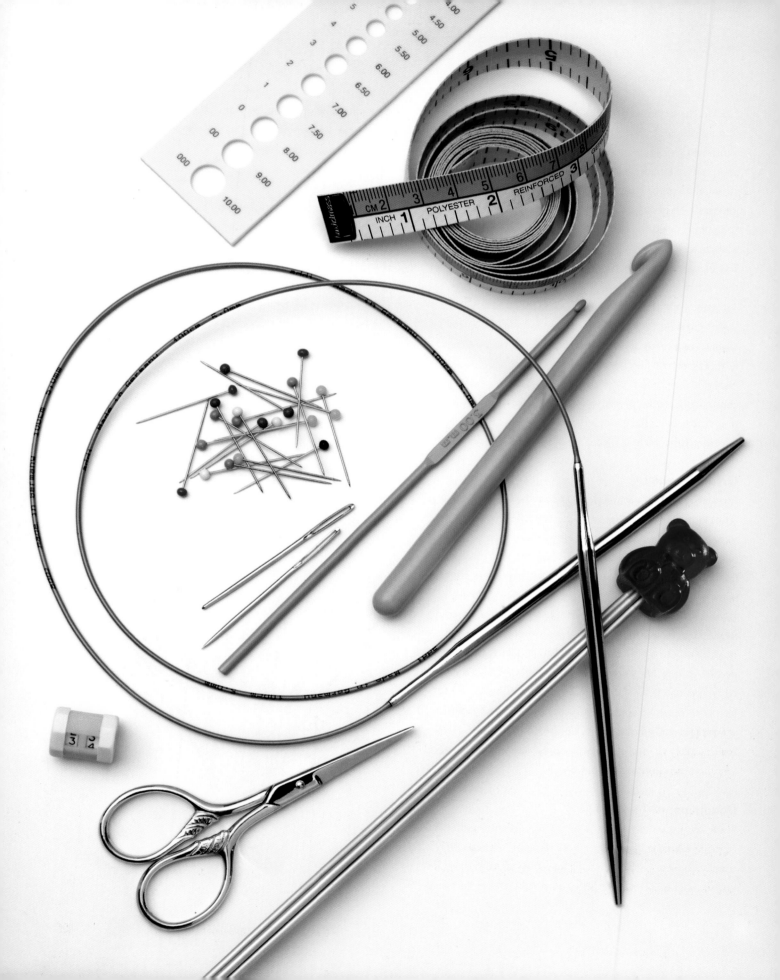

STITCH HOLDERS

These come in handy for holding stitches that you're not using. The safety-pin type works best, or use safety pins if you only have to hold a small number of stitches.

SEWING-UP NEEDLE

Buy a good yarn sewing-up needle with a big enough eye for the yarn you are using.

PINS

Dressmaking pins with coloured ends are used for blocking and checking tension. Ordinary dressmaking pins will get lost in the yarn.

ROW COUNTERS

These help you record your progress by turning the counter to the number you have reached when counting rows. This means that if you have to leave your knitting and get up for any reason you will know exactly which row you are on and can continue on your return. You are supposed to slide them to the bottom of your needle, but sometimes this feels uncomfortable when knitting with smaller needles as the counters can be a bit heavy. Try threading the row counter with a thick piece of yarn and wearing it as a necklace. It could catch on as a fashion statement and shows you are part of the knitting movement.

CROCHET HOOKS

Like knitting needles, crochet hooks come in different sizes. They are shorter than knitting needles and have a hook on one end. They are useful tools for of picking up the inevitable lost stitch or two.

NEEDLE PROTECTORS

These stop the stitches from falling off. Buy plenty of them – they're essential.

BUTTONS

Buttons can be a fabulous decoration and finish off your knitted piece to perfection. However, choose wisely. A cheap, unattractive button can undermine the quality of your garment. Make sure you choose the right size button for the buttonhole instructions in the pattern.

Buttons are made in all shapes and sizes and from many different materials: ceramic, glass, plastic, shell, metal, horn and wood. Check the washing instructions for the buttons, as unprotected metal ones may rust.

Buttons can be used to embellish bags, hats and cushions.

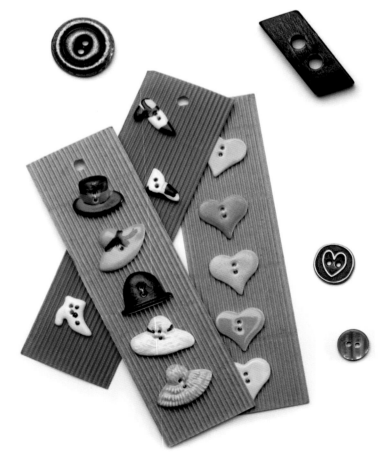

What you need… and what to do with it

Carrying and Storing Your Knitting

MAMA'S GOT A BRAND-NEW BAG

After you've been knitting a while, you may notice the whole house being taken over by end-bits of yarn: pieces that you can't bear to throw out because 'they might just come in useful one day'. So you'll need to find somewhere to store them.

Baskets are good, as they show off your wool and, if well placed, make them a design feature in an interior. If you don't want to show them off, plastic stackable boxes are another storage option. Click the lid tight if you're putting them in the cellar or a loft, as mice have been known to make comfy little nests in these wool havens. And besides, who wants to see a rat wearing the same cardigan as you? Moths can also attack yarn, so if you plan on leaving the yarn unattended for a long time, investment in a few mothballs may be wise.

What should you use to carry your knitting around? About the need to do this there is no question – you must take it out and show it off, in fact, treat it like a new boyfriend. You'll surely get more interest in the knitting than the boyfriend (excepting any Johnny Depp look-alikes, of course). For this you will need something deep enough to keep the needles from poking out and causing injury. So you need enough room in that bag to carry bits of your knitting equipment, it needs to complement your knitting and, naturally, it should be a very hip bag. Baskets work well, but don't get one that will snag the knitting; do check that the handles are strong enough. Another idea is to make your own – the bag on page 94 is perfect and simple to make.

And don't forget – you must make a point of knitting in public. So, rock on knitting… keep the revolution alive.

What you need… and what to do with it

Knitting Techniques

Holding your needles

Hold your needles in a cross position with the right needle behind the left. With your left hand, support both the needles using the left index finger at the back to support the right needle and the left thumb to pinch the left needle against the right one. In this way your right hand is free to work the yarn.

Having cast on (see page 30), hold the cast-on stitches on the left-hand needle. Hold the right-hand needle as you would a pen, but tilt it back slightly. Put the right-hand needle into the stitch, making sure the needles cross with the right needle behind the left. Put your left thumb on the left needle and your left index finger behind the cross so you are supporting the cross with a pinch action. Your right hand

should now be free to pick up the yarn. Your left thumb should be resting about 2.5cm (1in) from the tip of the needle.

Another holding method that some people find more comfortable involves holding the right needle in the same manner as the left, not as a pen but more like a dinner knife.

If you are holding long needles, tuck the right needle under your arm to keep it from flapping about. This is how my grandmother taught me to knit. It's certainly a useful tip if the man next to you on the train is reading a paper. Although tapping a paper rhythmically with your needles as you knit makes a wonderful sound – try it.

Holding your yarn

There is a trick to holding your yarn so that your tension isn't too tight or too loose. It seems that no two knitters hold their yarn in the same way. The method that I recommend is as follows:

Pick up the yarn with your right little finger, with your palm facing upwards so the yarn end joined to the ball is caught between your little finger and third finger. Turn your hand round towards you, twisting the yarn around your little finger (1).

Now, with your palm facing down, catch the yarn with your slightly pointed index finger, keeping the yarn held by bending your last three fingers inwards. Now hold the left needle (2).

This method keeps the yarn in place so you don't have to keep picking it up or dropping the needles for every stitch. Remember to hold the needles crossed and with a pinch from the left hand.

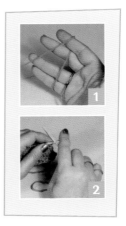

Casting on

The best way to learn to cast on is to be taught first hand. Lure a granny in from the street with the promise of tea, offer to bake them a cake for a good cause in return, or if all else fails, just a friend and a copy of this book will do! Then one of you can read the instructions while the other tackles the needles and yarn.

There are several methods of casting on; some methods give a stronger bottom edge than others, but every method starts with a slip knot. When casting on, make sure you keep the stitches loose.

CASTING ON WITH A SLIP KNOT – THE TWO-NEEDLE METHOD

The first stage to casting on is to make the first stitch by making a loop with a slip knot. Unwind the ball to give you approximately 30cm (12in) of yarn. Hold the yarn with your left hand with the tail hanging down and the ball of wool on your right.

With the right hand, wrap the yarn twice around your first two fingers, making a cross at the front in the middle of your fingers. Put the needle under the first loop (1), turn the needle so that it points down between your fingers, continue turning until the needle has done a 180 degree turn. Slip the loop off your fingers and on to the needle and, gently tighten the stitch (2).

CASTING ON THE REST OF YOUR STITCHES

Make sure the needle with the slip knot is in your left hand. Slide the right needle up through the stitch, so it sits behind and the needles are crossed. Take the yarn in your right hand and wrap around the right needle from the back to the front (3). Pull your right needle back so the point comes down and catches the loop you have just made (4). Slip the new stitch off the right needle on to the left needle.

Don't be put off if you see…

The Novice Knitter

  What you need… and what to do with it

How to knit a stitch

So, well done, by hook or by crook you've managed to cast on those stitches. Now you need to get down to the 'knitty gritty' and get going in earnest! Try putting on some music first. Knitting is just like playing an instrument. There are four moves to every knit stitch, so it's like a four-time beat.

As you knit, just keep on repeating 'In, Round, Through and Off'. Forget any mantras you were given at meditation classes and repeat this knitting chant instead.

IN (1):
Hold the yarn at the back. Slide the point of the right needle through the first loop, taking the tip of the right-hand needle so it sits in a cross behind the left.

ROUND (2):
Hold the needles with your left hand in a pinch. Pick up the yarn with your right hand and wrap it anti-clockwise round from the back of the right needle, through the middle of the cross. The yarn should now be at the front.

THROUGH (3):
Slide the right needle down and back through the stitch, making a loop on the right needle.

OFF (4):
Slip the original stitch off the left needle, leaving the newly formed stitch on the right needle.

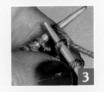

How to purl a stitch

IN (1):
Hold the yarn at the front. Slide the right needle through the first stitch on the left needle from right to left, taking the tip of the right-hand needle across in front of the left.

ROUND (2):
Using your right forefinger, take the yarn around the right needle in an anti-clockwise direction through the middle of the cross.

THROUGH (3):
Slide the right needle back up through the stitch, catching the yarn to create a loop on the right needle.

OFF (4):
Slip the original stitch off the left needle, leaving the newly formed stitch on the right needle.

At the end of every row, whether knit or purl, you will need to turn your work so you can start the next row. Hold the needle with all the stitches on the left, leaving the right needle empty ready for you to begin the next row.

How to slip a stitch

In some patterns you will be required to slip a stitch. This is a method of passing a stitch from one needle to the other without knitting it.

With the right needle, using your IN chant, slip the right needle into the stitch on the left needle either 'knitwise' or 'purlwise' and OFF on to the right needle.

Garter stitch

This is created by using the knit stitch on every row. This produces an elastic piece of fabric and a construction that is perfect for learning to knit. Knitting a garter-stitch scarf (see page 78) for yourself or for the man in your life is an ideal first knitting project.

Stocking stitch

This is the most common stitch. Whether knitting a jumper in one colour or knitting a complicated Fairisle design, most patterns will be based on this stitch. Stocking stitch consists of one row of knit and one row of purl. This produces a flat fabric with the stitches of your work looking like little 'v's, and makes counting stitches easy, as each 'v' makes one stitch.

When you are knitting stocking stitch, on a knit row you will have the little 'v's facing you and when you turn your work to purl, the little bumps on the other side will be facing you.

Right or wrong side?

The 'right' side of your work will have the 'v's and the 'wrong' side will have the bumps. This is important to remember when coming to the end of your garment, when the next stage is to sew it up.

Right side *Wrong side*

What you need... and what to do with it

Rib

A classic-style jumper has a rib at the bottom and on the cuffs. Rib is more elastic than stocking stitch and it will keep its shape better.

Ribbing consists of a sequence of knit and purl stitches in one row. The most common type of rib for cuffs and edgings is knit 1 st, purl 1 st and so on until the end of the row. Knit 2 sts, purl 2 sts makes a very elastic rib and is commonly used for scarves and hats. This stitch gives shaping to a garment that is designed to cling and show curves.

When ribbing, you need to remember to put your yarn to the back of your knitting for the knit stitch and bring it forward again for the purl stitch.

How to increase and decrease

Until you learn how to increase and decrease, you will be stuck with a square piece of fabric, which is only useful for scarves and blankets. So, to get to do those funky styles and garments that are shaped to fit the natural human form, you will have to shape up!

Remember that your arms are thinner at the bottom and wider at the top and the top of your torso is wider than your waist (well, sometimes!). Even a simple hat has to decrease at the top, unless some of you have square heads.

Increasing is usually done on the right side of the work. Patterns do not always give instructions on how to increase, as there are several methods. Increasing is also known as 'making a stitch'.

SIMPLE INCREASE

The simplest method is to work into the front and back of the same stitch. On a knit row, knit the stitch in, round and through, but don't take the stitch off (1). Instead, take the right needle, with the loop still on the left needle, and knit into the back of the stitch on the left needle (2). Slip the stitch off. You have now created an extra stitch.

On a purl row, purl into the front of the stitch as normal, but don't take the loop off the left needle. Purl into the back of the stitch on the left needle, creating the extra stitch.

SIMPLE DECREASE

The easiest way to decrease is by knitting or purling two stitches together at the same time. On a knit row, slide the right needle up through two stitches and knit them together as one stitch (3). This is called knit two together and is abbreviated in a pattern as k2tog. Use the same method for purling, only purl two stitches together.

Increasing

Decreasing

Casting off (binding off)

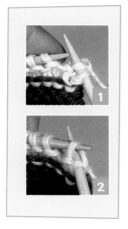

When casting off, you will usually be casting off an edge where you will pick up the stitches afterwards either to sew up or to make into a neckline. This means that it is vital to cast off loosely.

Knit the first two stitches on to the right-hand needle (1). Take the first stitch over the second, leaving one stitch on the needle (2). Knit the next stitch and draw the stitch already on the needle over it.

Always try to cast off on a knit row, but if you need to do it on a purl row, take the yarn back when you slip the second stitch over the first stitch and bring it back again to purl the next stitch.

When you get to the very last stitch, break the yarn, take the last stitch off the needle, thread the yarn through the loop and tighten.

If you need a really elastic cast-off edge, cast off in rib (1 stitch knit followed by 1 stitch purl).

Knitting a tension square

Once you have chosen your pattern, yarn and needles, the knitting drug will compel you to get started as soon as possible. But no matter how eager you feel, you must first knit a tension swatch. This determines the finished measurements of your garment. Many mistakes have been made owing to the lack of a swatch and the most beautiful garments have been passed over to the cat or dog basket because they are either too large or too small. Most patterns and yarn will give an ideal gauge.

Use the same needles, yarn and stitch as the pattern and knit a sample of at least 12.5cm (5in) square. Smooth out the piece on a flat surface without stretching it. Place a ruler horizontally on the work and mark 10cm (4in) with pins. Count the number of stitches between the pins. To check the row tension, put the ruler vertically on the work and mark 10cm (4in) with the pins. If you find you have more stitches or rows than the gauge in your pattern suggests, knit another swatch using larger needles, or if it is less try again with smaller needles.

6 Fashionable girls are turning to old-fashioned hobbies to ease the strain of urban life. Now knitting has replaced networking as the hippest after-hours occupation. 9

Vogue, May 2004

Joining yarn and changing colours

At some point the ball of wool will run out and you will need to join yarn. Whenever possible, join in new yarn at the beginning of a row. To measure if you have enough yarn to finish a row, measure across the row with the remaining yarn. If it reaches four times across the width, you will have enough for a stocking-stitch row.

Slide your right needle into the first stitch. Place the new yarn over the old yarn and bring it between the two needles with the tail end to the left side. Make sure you leave a tail approximately 10cm (4in) long.

Bring your yarn up from under the existing yarn and knit with the new yarn, so that both types of yarn have twisted together at the back. Make sure you leave sufficient yarn to sew in.

After you've done a few stitches, stop and tie the ends in a knot – they can be sewn into the seam later.

Don't be put off if you see…

The Urban Boho

How to read a knitting pattern

Once you've tuned into the knitting lingo, it's just like following a cookery recipe. But let's dismiss that analogy in case you knit a cabbage jumper. Like a recipe, however, always read the pattern through first so you get an idea of how the design and techniques fit into place.

The beginning of each pattern will have the sizing and the materials you need to knit with.

SIZING

The smallest sizes of the item you're knitting will be printed first and the larger sizes will follow on.

To fit bust:					
81	86	91	97	102	cm
32	34	36	38	40	in

Just to confuse things, you will sometimes be given the actual size measurement of the garment. This is the actual size that it will knit to, rather than the measurement of the person who will be wearing it. Remember that most knitted garments won't be as tight-fitting as a bra, so you will need a bit of space to get into it. Following the size, you will have the measurement of the garment's length and its sleeve seam length. Remember that if you need to adjust the length, you may need extra yarn.

Bust measurement: the measurement of the bust/chest is taken under the arms. Ask someone you fancy to help you out – it's good for breaking the ice on a first date.

Back measurement: this is the length from the back of the neck to the very bottom edge of the garment.

Sleeve measurement: this is from the edge of the cuff to the widest point, which is just below your armpit.

The pattern may show these measurements in a diagram.

MATERIALS

Yarn amounts are also shown at the beginning of the pattern, underneath the measurements so you can calculate the amount of yarn needed to knit the pattern.

To fit bust:					
81	86	91	97	102	cm
32	34	36	38	40	in
Yarn:					
10	10	11	12	13	balls

Make quite sure you have bought the correct amount of yarn and if you are substituting a yarn, make sure it has the equivalent weight, metreage or yardage. Sometimes it's wise to overbuy a little to avoid running out of yarn. Most good yarn suppliers will let you have a refund on unopened balls or hanks of wool. If you have an accommodating supplier, they may be able to put yarn aside for you and you can buy it as and when you need it. This ensures you get the right dye-lot number for the yarn you have chosen. (Don't expect them to keep it for the jumper that you've been working on for the past 18 years, though.)

  What you need… and what to do with it

In the materials section of the pattern you will also find the recommended needle size and any other equipment that's needed, such as buttons, beads, cable needles, crochet hooks or stitch holders.

KNITTING INSTRUCTIONS YARDAGE

It can sometimes be confusing to read through the pattern before you begin. This is because it will only become obvious once you start knitting, so don't start thinking you're totally dumb or that the pattern is useless!

Knitting instructions give the smallest size first and the larger sizes follow within brackets. So, for example, cast on 96 (100: 106: 110: 116). Follow the order according to the size you are knitting throughout. It's useful to go through the pattern with a highlighter marker pen so you don't read the wrong size by mistake.

Asterisks or brackets are used to indicate the repetition of a sequence of stitches. So, for example, '*K1, p2; rep from * to end' means that you must repeat the sequence inside the asterisks until you get to the end of the row. This instruction can also be written in brackets, as '(K1, p2) to end'. To confuse you even more, asterisks and brackets are sometimes used together. For example '*K1, p2 (K2, p1) 3 times; rep from * to end'. The bracket instruction means that these stitches only are to be repeated three times before returning to the instructions immediately after the asterisk. So, following the example, you knit 1, pearl 2 and then knit 2 and pearl 1 three times, and then go back to the beginning of the sequence until the end of the row. Confused? Well, just start knitting and it will become more obvious.

It is always good to have a pencil in hand to make sure you repeat the sequence the exact number of times specified. Some knitters have a pin neatly attached to the pattern page and make little points instead of pencil marks.

If you have to put your knitting down in a hurry to answer the phone or the doorbell, always take the time to mark where you are on the pattern or you will end up having to take the row back because you've forgotten where you are. The salesman at the door isn't worth losing stitches over.

The phrase 'work straight' means continue knitting without increasing or decreasing, until instructed.

'COZ MAKING UP IS HARD TO DO

Making up is always a good thing. Sometimes over a cup of tea or a romantic meal, but in knitting terms it means putting the whole thing together. Always follow the recommended sequence in the pattern; it will be there for a reason (see page 43 for sewing-up instructions).

ABBREVIATIONS

The next hurdle is to understand the pattern abbreviations. They are not as bad as they look. You won't need to memorise them because they are usually at the beginning or the end of most pattern books. You will find them at the beginning of the patterns section (see page 55).

> ' *Knitting, if you choose, can be at the heart of a fulfilling and creative way of living.* '
>
> *Weekend Knitting: 50 Unique Projects and Ideas*

Fairisle patterns

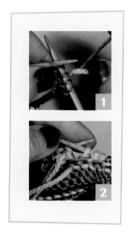

Fairisle is the technique used for working with more than one colour. At some point you just won't be able to resist having a go, as there are so many wonderful patterns that you can add to your knitting repertoire. So don't be scared of the big 'F' word, Fairisle.

Fairisle takes a little more concentration than one-colour knitting, so turn off the TV, allow yourself a spot of time and don't answer the phone. Fairisle works better in stocking stitch where the design shows at the front of the work and the yarn is carried along at the back.

In most knitting instruction manuals the Fairisle techniques 'stranding' and 'weaving' are explained. These explanations can be enough to drive any novice knitter to the nearest bonfire to burn their bamboo needles, so some easier methods are outlined here.

OVER AND UNDER

If you are knitting a design that has less than four stitches in one colour, use the over-and-under method.

So, for example:
1. Knit with the first colour yarn.
2. When you want to bring in a new colour, drop the first colour and bring the 2nd colour over the 1st colour and start knitting with it.

Your yarns can get very tangled as they wind around themselves and it can take just as much time untangling yarn as it does knitting the garment, so if you alternate the over and under to under and over every time you do a colour change, you'll find the yarn gets less messed up. There are several tips to keeping colours from

tangling. Some people divide the balls of yarn and put them into separate jam jars. I find you still have to move the jam jars around all over the place and then as soon as you move for a cup of tea you knock them over and spend all your time chasing the balls around the room, putting them back in the jars.

TWISTING

If you are knitting with more than three stitches use the twisting method, this is the best method for carrying along the colour you're not using. It also keeps the knitting from getting too tight and puckering up.

Knit with the first colour yarn (colour A). Join in the 2nd colour (colour B) (1). After 2 or 3 stitches, pick up yarn A and twist it around yarn B at the back and continue knitting with yarn B. Just keep twisting when you want to change colours. In this way your yarn will be carried behind the work and will avoid forming long loops (the pieces of yarn that get carried behind your work) (2). The loops can look ugly if too long and can catch in fingers or hands. If you twist on every stitch, your work will bunch up and look ugly. If you twist every three stitches, your work will lay flat and still allow the fabric to stretch.

When you get to the end of a row, just before your last stitch, twist your yarn so your second colour extends to the end of the row.

HOW TO READ A FAIRISLE PATTERN

The easy answer is 'carefully'. Most Fairisle patterns are worked from a chart, which can take a bit of getting used to. Choose a simple design in two colours to start off with (such as the mobile phone/iPod cover on page 74).

A chart will give a single pattern repeat of the complete design on a squared grid. Either colours or symbols will represent the colours. Work from the bottom to the top. Horizontally, each square represents a stitch and vertically each square represents a row.

For a stocking-stitch pattern:
Knit rows – read the chart from right to left.
Purl rows – read the chart from left to right.

When you have completed one row, follow the row that is immediately above the last. Keep a pencil or a row counter near by and mark off the rows as you complete them.

Often, only one repeat of the pattern is shown and you will have to repeat this pattern across the row. There will be bold vertical lines to show the area that is to be repeated. The stitches at either side of these lines show the edge stitches to be worked at the beginning and the end of the work.

Follow the pattern exactly. I'll repeat that: follow the pattern exactly. And for those of you looking after young children: follow the pattern exactly. Constantly check your work after every few stitches and every row. If you have gone wrong, don't continue in the hope it will work out. It won't. Undo the incorrect stitches and correct the mistakes.

Don't be put off if you see…

The country living knitter

Troubleshooting — or the knitting-disaster hall of fame

Here is a quick problem-solving guide to common mistakes when knitting.

'OOPS, I'VE DROPPED A STITCH'

It's so easy to do. Everyone does it, so it is essential that you know how to pick up dropped stitches.

Picking up stitches on a knit row

Hold your knitting with the right side (knit side) facing (1). Put the tip of the right needle into the dropped stitch from front to back, to stop it running any further. Then pick up the horizontal strand of yarn, so it sits above the stitch (2). With your left needle, lift the picked-up stitch over the horizontal strand and slip it off the needle (3). Transfer the stitch on to the left needle (4).

Picking up stitches on a purl row

Hold your knitting with the wrong side (purl side) facing (5). Put the tip of the right needle into the dropped stitch from back to front. Pick up the horizontal strand of yarn, so it sits above the stitch (6). With your left needle, lift the picked-up stitch over the horizontal strand and slip it off the needle (7). Transfer the stitch on to the left needle (8).

LADDERS

If the dropped stitch creates a ladder going down several rows, either pick up the stitch in the usual way, picking up from the bottom to the top, or instead use a crochet hook.

Work with the dropped stitch at the front of the knitting (9). Put the crochet hook into the stitch from front to back. Loop the horizontal strand with the crochet hook and pull it through the stitch (10). Continue up the ladder and when you reach the top, hook the stitch on to the left needle – then you can cheer.

TWIST AND SHOUT, OR TWISTED STITCHES

Twisted stitches are created either when dropped stitches have been picked up the wrong way round or when the yarn has been taken the wrong way round the needle.

On a knit row: knit into the back of the stitch.
On a purl row: purl into the back of the stitch.

 What you need... and what to do with it

UNDOING STITCHES

This is always a frustrating activity. Having gone to all the time and trouble knitting, the last thing you want is to have to unravel it. It's a bit like taking the wrong turning up the motorway and having to drive 10 miles to the next junction and 20 miles back to get to where you wanted.

Undoing stitches stitch by stitch

If your mistake is on the same row or only one row down, you may need to unravel your knitting stitch by stitch.

Put your yarn at the back with the right side facing you. Put the left needle from front to back through the stitch below the stitch you want to unravel that's on the right needle (1). Pull the right needle back and let the stitch slip off the needle and pull the yarn (2).

For a purl row, you should use the same method but with the wrong side facing and the yarn at the front.

Unravelling rows

Try to avoid this, but you may need to take off several rows if you have failed to correct a mistake by picking up individual stitches.

Put your knitting on a flat surface and pull the needle away and off the stitches. With one hand on the knitting to keep it flat, pull the yarn with the other hand and gently undo the amount of rows needed. Make sure you count the rows and allow for any decreasing or increasing that you have made. Deduct the rows off your row counter.

When you have undone as many rows as required, put the stitches back on the needle with a smaller size needle. Start knitting again as normal, using your original size needles.

WHAT ROW AM I ON?

Even though the house may be completely quiet and you are convinced you won't be disturbed, there will inevitably come a moment when you will innocently put your knitting down. Then, when you get back to it, you'll have to work out what row you were on.

This is where the importance of the classic knitters' phrase, 'I've just got to finish this row!' comes into play. When you put your work down in the middle of a row, it's an easy mistake to pick it up and start knitting the wrong way. Always make sure your yarn is on the right of your work and try to finish a row before going off to make the tea or answering the phone (and remember to mark on your pattern the stage you have reached!).

If you do lose your place, when you pick up the knitting again hold your two needles and see where your yarn is. Whether it's at the front or the back, it should always be worked with the yarn coming from the top stitch on the right needle. If the yarn is coming out from the left needle, simply turn the knitting around and continue your work.

Picking up stitches for borders

To prevent the edge of the knitted fabric from curling, most knitted pieces will have an edging or border, either sewn on or created by picking up stitches. In the pattern instructions this may be referred to as 'pick up and knit' or 'knit up'. The pattern will tell you how many stitches are to be picked up.

PICKING UP ON A CAST-ON/CAST-OFF EDGE USING ONE NEEDLE

With the right side facing you, put the right needle from the front to the back under both loops (1). Wind the yarn round the needle and in a knit action draw the loop through to create a new stitch on the needle (2). Continue to pick up the amount of stitches specified in the pattern.

PICKING UP ALONG A SIDE EDGE

With the right side facing and with one needle in your right hand, pick up the stitches one stitch in from the edge. This ensures a neater edge and keeps your work tidy.

It is useful to mark out the number of stitches you need evenly along the length of fabric with pins. Measure the distance along the edge and divide it by the number of stitches you are instructed to pick up.

Knitting buttonholes

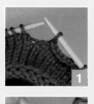

Buttonholes on knitted garments do not always create the neatest of holes. This doesn't matter, however, as you can neaten them with a blanket stitch later. The fun is in choosing the buttons to pretty up your knitted item.

Knit until you get to the part in the pattern where you need the buttonhole. Cast off the amount of stitches specified in the pattern (this depends on the size of the buttonhole and the thickness of your yarn) (1). Knit to the end of the row. On your next row, knit to the point where your cast-off stitches are. Turn your work by switching your needles; put the left needle in the right hand and the right needle in the left hand. Cast on the same number of stitches as you cast off. Turn your work again and work to the end (2).

Sewing in ends

If possible, sew in the yarn ends as you go along and certainly before you make up the garment, otherwise you'll end up with all the loose ends tangled up in the seams as you're sewing up. Thread the loose end into a yarn-sewing needle. Sew in and out through the bars of the stitch on the wrong side of the work and cut them loosely so the yarn doesn't unravel. Stitches can be darned either vertically or horizontally, whichever looks neater. If you ignore this advice, the back of your garment will end up looking like a hedgehog's bed.

Sewing up or making up

This can also be called 'knitting, sewing and kittens…' Once you've knitted your garment, you then need to sew it together, but you're having kittens at the thought… At this point I used to just hand my knitted pieces over to my mother, so I never felt the satisfaction of finishing it all by myself. She eventually got fed up and made me sew up on my own. Many knitters give up just before it comes to sewing up, throw the knitted pieces together in a bag and abandon it in the loft. But don't panic, it's incredibly satisfying to see the pieces all coming together, so just take your time and breathe…

Place the pieces on a flat surface, putting them next to each other so you can see the shape of the garment, right side up. Pin the pieces together very loosely. Safety pins are more suitable than dressmakers' pins, which tend to get lost in the knitted fabric. Pin the corners first and fill in the other bits after. Keep checking and double-checking that you have it all the right way round, as the most frustrating thing is to start sewing and find that you have sewn a right side to a wrong side and a wrong side to a right side. Use the same yarn as your knitted fabric for the sewing up, unless it's a particularly weak or bulky yarn, in which case match up the colour with a thinner and stronger yarn.

> ❛Mrs Moon
> sitting up in the sky
> little old lady
> rock-a-bye
> with a ball of fading light
> and silvery needles
> knitting the night
>
> Mother by Prabha Raj
> As a pair of needles
> Criss cross,
> I see her thoughts
> Setting her wrinkles
> To play.
>
> The moment she completes
> The picking of stitches,
> Her wrinkles
> Erase out
>
> I call it
> The juxtaposition of
> Mind and sentiment.❜

Roger McGough, Mrs Moon

SEWING SEAMS

There are a number of techniques for joining seams. Start with the over-and-over method and try the others later when you are more confident.

Over-and-over method

This is the easiest method of joining seams, although not always the neatest. It gives a nice flat seam.

Thread sufficient yarn to sew up the whole seam. Put right side to right side, with a wrong side facing you. Starting at the bottom edge, put the needle from the back of your two pieces of fabric to the front. Take the needle over to the back and put the needle from back to front into the next stitch. Go back to the original first stitch and put the needle from back to front and pull it through. This secures the first stitch (1). Match corresponding stitches from both sides, put the needle into the top of the stitches through both pieces of fabric from the back and pull through to the front. Take the needle over and put in again from the back to the front as before. Continue by spacing the stitches approximately every two rows (2).

Beginning a seam for back stitch and mattress stitch

These are the first few stitches that hold the fabric together and secure the yarn so the sewing doesn't come undone.

Begin by putting both fabrics right side to right side, with the wrong side facing you. Use the long tail left from your cast-on row, or thread another piece of yarn into your sewing needle. Put the needle from back to front through the corner stitch of both pieces of knitting. Secure the yarn by putting the needle back up through the same hole (3).

Back stitch

This, the simplest of all sewing-up stitches, is suitable for seams and for yarn up to double-knitting thickness. This method produces a neat seam, but it can be bulky if used with thicker yarn.

Pin the right sides together with the wrong side facing you, pinning the sides together row for row (4). Begin your seam (as above), with the yarn finishing at the front. Put the needle into the work just behind where the last stitch came out and make a short stitch, bringing the needle back to the front (5). Put the needle back into where the previous stitch ended and make a long stitch, so the needle comes out about a stitch in front of where the last stitch ended (6). Keep repeating this process until the end. It will make a continuous line of stitches of a similar length on the side of the work facing you.

> 6 Knit on, with confidence and hope, through all crises. 9
>
> *Elizabeth Zimmermann*

Mattress stitch on stocking stitch

This is one of the neatest stitches to use. It takes a bit longer, but its almost invisible and makes a completely straight seam.

Begin your seam. With the right sides of your knitting facing each other, put your needle under the first two running bars and pull it through. (The bars are the pieces of yarn between each 'v' shape on the knit side (1).) Pass the needle under the first two bars on the other piece of fabric and pull it through. Don't pull your fabrics too close together at this point and leave your stitches quite loose – you will pull them together later (2). Put the needle into the same place that it came out of on the right-hand piece of fabric. Pick up the next two running bars, put the needle to the same point where it came out on the left-hand piece of fabric and come up two bars on the same side (3). When you have sewn 4 or 5 stitches, gently pull your yarn to draw the edges together and it will become invisible (4).

Joining two cast-off edges

This is a slight variation on mattress stitch and also creates a neat seam.

Begin your seam. With the right sides facing and working from right to left, put the needle through the centre of your first stitch underneath the cast-off stitch and pull it through. At this stage, don't pull your stitches tight, as this will be done later (5). Put your needle through the centre of the stitch corresponding on the opposite side and bring it out in the centre of the next stitch along (6). Put the needle into the centre of the next stitch along on the other side and back up through the centre of the next stitch along (7). Repeat until the end of the seam. When you have sewn 4 stitches, pull gently in the same way as with mattress stitch (8).

Washing, blocking and steaming (finishing your project)

Pressing your fabric can make the difference between it looking like a professional piece of art or an old rag you've found in a skip.

Yarn that has a high content of natural fibre can be pressed, but some yarn can be totally ruined by a hot iron. Check the label on the yarn for details of whether your yarn can be pressed. It should give you all the information you need, even the temperature at which the iron should be set. It will also tell you if you need to use a dry cloth or a damp cloth. Often you will find pressing instructions at the end of your pattern.

DAMP FINISHING

If you are instructed that the yarn is not to be pressed, then follow the method below.

Find a damp and colourfast towel (not the one you've just used for drying the dog). Lay your pieces of fabric on the damp towel and then roll them up loosely together. Leave for approximately one hour for the knitting to absorb the dampness from the towel.

Undo the towel on a flat surface and place the pieces once more on top of it. Pin the pieces into shape (this is blocking).

Find another damp cloth and lay it over the top so your fabric is sandwiched. Press gently down on to your fabric so every part is touching the cloth and leave it to dry somewhere where it's not going to stay damp for too long – otherwise it will start to smell.

BLOCKING

This is a method used to keep your garment in shape while it is drying. Blocking is sometimes also used to pin a garment out before sewing it up, especially when some knitted fabrics are prone to curling at the edges. It is a good way of shaping motifs and Fairisle, which can look uneven occasionally.

It's best to get as much moisture out of the knitted fabric as possible before laying it out. You can wrap it in a towel and then put it in the washing machine for a very short spin. Alternatively, wrap the item in a towel and press it gently to absorb as much water into the towel as possible. This is a great method for getting rid of any lingering angst, but don't press it too tight. Remember that you're only getting rid of excess water!

Before you start blocking, remember how the piece is supposed to look. Reshape the

pieces and lay them out on a dry towel. Pin out your pieces with large-headed coloured pins or large safety pins. Use a padded surface or, failing that, a nice thick towel. Gently ease the fabric into place to get the correct measurements and lay on the wrong side. Place the pins approximately 2.5cm (1in) apart on the very edge of the fabric.

PRESSING

Pressing helps the fabric hold its shape. The label should give you pressing instructions. As a rule, any natural yarn and cotton and linen can be pressed with a damp cloth. Steam irons are also an asset, as they can be used over a cloth and don't need to actually touch the knitting so won't flatten it in any way. Synthetic yarn should not be pressed. For yarn mixtures that have some natural and some synthetic fibres, press with a cool iron over a dry cloth. However, never use steam on acrylic, as it goes 'dead' and sloppy. A great investment is a Teflon or non-stick cover for your iron that makes it glide over the knitting, allowing the steam to come out of the iron without scorching. Turn on the iron and check the correct temperature. Place the damp or dry cloth over

Blocking – before

Blocking – after

  What you need… and what to do with it

the pinned-out pieces of knitting. Hover the iron over the damp cloth so it makes it steam; don't drag the iron over the fabric or it will become misshapen. Do not press any ribbed edges. Remove some of the pins and, if the work stays flat, take the rest of the pins out and leave to dry. If the edges are still curling when you have taken some of the pins out, you need to repin it and leave it to dry with the pins in. Once you have finished sewing up your garment, press it again along the seams using the same method, only this time without any pinning.

WASHING

Washing a hand-knitted garment can be a terrifying thought when you have other clothes that have been tinted with dye that has run in the wash. And the last thing you need is to spend all that tender loving care on knitting and finishing your garment, only to have it shrink to such a minute state that you have to donate it to the elves' section of a charity shop.

The most important thing is to read the yarn label. This tends to read like a cryptic code, so a few hints follow to help you out.

Hand-washing

Use lukewarm water and a mild soap washing agent. There are various liquid handwashing products on the market and I prefer to use these as the powder takes more time to dissolve and some don't dissolve so well in mild temperatures. Don't rub the knitted fabric, but gently squeeze it to loosen any dirt. Do not leave your knitted garment to soak – it's best to get it washed and dried in the shortest possible time. Let the water out of the sink before lifting the garment out and gently squeeze the water out when the sink is empty.

The garment may be very heavy when filled with water and lifting it out of the water may stretch it. Lay the garment on a towel and roll it up loosely. Then take another towel, lay the garment out and reshape the garment to its correct measurements. Leave the piece to dry naturally away from direct sunlight, and don't be tempted to put it on the radiator.

Note: You can spin some knitted yarn, such as cotton and linen, in the washing machine on a slow and gentle cycle.

Machine washing

Check the yarn label to find out if your yarn is machine washable. Use the instructions and set the machine on the recommended temperature. If you are nervous about the item stretching, put the item in a pillowcase inside the drum of the machine. In times of extreme agitation, revert to handwashing! Then lay out the garment to dry. Don't put it in the tumble dryer.

Dry cleaning

If the label says 'dry clean', dry clean only. Make sure your dry cleaner doesn't put it on a hanger and doesn't press it. Take the yarn label in for them to check. Remember, this is your masterpiece.

> ❛ *In the rhythm of the needles, there is music for the soul.* ❜
>
> *Text from a sampler*

Beading

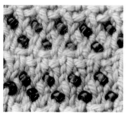

Beading can make the difference between a well-executed and worthy piece of knitting and a really jazzed-up little number. It can give a real quality finish to cuffs and borders and can make bags and purses look delectably classy.

Threading beads on to the yarn is a fairly complicated activity, but a strangely satisfying one. You may imagine that you can just thread them straight on to the yarn needle and then straight on to the yarn… but think again. Most beads don't have a huge hole and won't go on the yarn needle, so first of all find yourself a thin cotton-sewing needle.

Make sure you buy beads that have a big enough hole to fit on a cotton-sewing needle. You'll be surprised at the size of bead holes once you start looking and some people can get quite obsessed about it. If you find yourself mumbling 'Hmmm… precioussssss' in triumph and delight when you find the right one, just like Golum in *The Lord of the Rings*, it's time to seek medical help.

THREADING BEADS

This needs to be done before you start knitting. Double-thread your cotton-sewing needle with a piece of cotton thread so the loop hangs down. Then thread your yarn through the loop, leaving a tail approximately 15cm (6in) long. Thread the bead over the needle and push it down to the end of the cotton until you get to the yarn, then continue to push it over the yarn beyond the tail until it is on a single yarn thread.

Thread as many beads as you require on to the yarn. It is better to thread more than you need rather than less, because once you start knitting you can't add more beads without breaking the yarn and rethreading them (1).

There are several methods for knitting with beads; this one seems most logical, and once you get started it all becomes obvious.

Knit to the point where the bead is required. Put the right needle into the stitch. Bring one of the beads up the yarn until it meets the work, so it is in position (2). Knit into the next stitch and push the bead through the stitch to the right side of your work (3). Pull the yarn firmly in place (4).

On a purl row, repeat the method as for the knit row, but push the bead through to the right side.

Dazzling Decorations

All knitters have bags or baskets full of end-bits of yarn left over from the previous project – and some knitting magpies also keep hoards of beads. Don't let these valuable materials go to waste; they can make a huge difference to a plain piece of knitting. The following decorations are perfect fun items to adorn your cushions, jumpers, bags, hats or scarves.

What you need… and what to do with it

Pom-poms

Pom-poms can liven up a cushion, throw, hat, scarf or dog jacket. Try using strands of yarn different colours to make multi-coloured ones. When you have used up one colour, just change to a different colour.

Cut out two circles of card (an empty cereal packet will do nicely) to the size you want your pom-pom to be, using a glass or other circular utensil as a guide (1). Cut a small hole in the centre of each circle (2). Place the two circles together. Wind some wool off a ball to make a small ball. Put the tail through the small circle and start winding it round the cards through the hole, until the hole is so small that you can't get any more wool through (3). For a thinner pom-pom, use less wool. When the last piece of yarn is used up, with both index fingers pull the yarn apart at the outer circle to reveal the card. Insert scissors between the two pieces of card. Holding the tail of yarn with your left hand, cut round the outer edge of the pom-pom (4). When you have cut all the way round, wind a separate piece of yarn between the two pieces of card. Secure very tightly in a double knot (5). Remove the two cards and trim the pom-pom.

Don't be put off if you see…

The hippy knitter

Tassels

These look great on the corners of cushions or on the top of hats.

Find a cassette or CD case, or something solid the required length of the tassel. Wrap your yarn round the CD case 30 or 40 times, depending on the thickness of the wool and how fat you want the tassel to be (1). Cut the yarn at the bottom. Take a separate piece of yarn and thread it through the top of the wool on the CD case. Tie very tight with a double knot (2). Pull all the wool off the CD case. Holding the top of the tassel with your left hand, take some scissors and cut the bottom to form tassels (3).

Cut a separate piece of yarn. Tie the yarn around the tassel and make a neck, wrapping the yarn round the tassel several times. Secure with a double knot (4). Thread the same piece of yarn on a sewing needle and push the needle from front to back several times to secure (5). Trim the bottom.

Fringes

Fringes are perfect for scarves or any other garment to give them a more glamorous appearance.

Find a cassette or CD case, or something solid the required length of the fringe. Wrap your yarn round the CD case 4 or 5 times, depending on the thickness of the wool and how fat you want the fringe to be (1).

Slide the wool off the CD case, holding it tightly at the top. Push the fringe up through the bottom loop of the knitted item, using either your fingers or a crochet hook (2). Making a loop with the fringe, push the bottom of the tassel though it and pull tight (3). Trim the bottom.

What you need... and what to do with it

Knitted bow

This pretty bow (below) is made from five pieces of ribbed knitting.

Make the two loops from two pieces of ribbing 22 sts wide and 14cm (5$\frac{1}{2}$in) long. The two pointed ends are made by casting on 2 sts and then increasing in the first stitch of every other row until 22 sts are on the needle. Then knit straight until the end measures 14cm (5$\frac{1}{2}$in). The middle strap is made with 16 sts and 6.5cm (2$\frac{1}{2}$in) of ribbed knitting. (K1, P1).

To make up, fold the pieces for the loops in half, pleat them so they look neat and sew them securely. Pleat the straight ends of the pointed pieces and sew to the loops. Wrap the small strip to form the knot and the bow is complete.

Knitted flower

Knit this flower with any yarn, using the needles recommended for the yarn. It can be used to add extra glamour to bags, hats and scarves – or simply put a safety pin in the back and use it as a brooch.

Cast on 8 sts.
Row 1: slip 1, knit 7
Row 2: slip 1, knit 5 (2 sts remain on left needle), turn and put yarn to the back.
Row 3: slip 1, knit 3 (2 sts remain on left needle), turn and put yarn to the back.
Row 4: slip 1, knit 3, turn.
Row 5: slip 1, knit 5 (0 sts remain on left needle), turn.
Row 6: slip 1, knit 6 (leaving 1 st on left needle), turn.
Row 7: slip 1 and begin casting off until 1 st remains, turn.
Cast on 7 sts.

Repeat 5 times (to create 6 petals).
Cast off last sts leaving a long tail.
Thread tail on a wool-sewing needle and sew first petal to last petal creating a flower shape. Weave sewing needle in and out of each petal along inside edge of hole and gently pull yarn together, closing hole.
Sew in ends.

PART THREE

Patterns...

...Funky Fashions

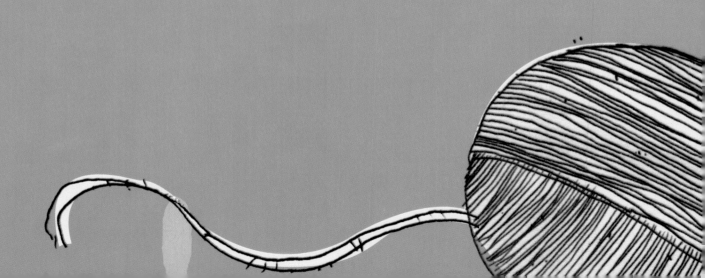

Keeping Up with the Bridget Joneses

Because we all now lead such pressured, busy lives, knitting activities are most popularly focused on quick projects that can easily be accommodated between other commitments.

In the patterns section that follows (see pages 56–97), projects have been chosen that use basic but interesting techniques and that incorporate the new attractive yarns that have played a strong part in drawing knitters back to the craft over the past few years. Yarns have been selected from fashionable yarn suppliers who have responded to the fact that new knitters are constantly inspired by yarn colour and variety and so consequently change and update the yarns on offer in order to meet new trends in knitting. You'll find chunky knits and cottons from Rowan; hand-dyed chunky, ribbon and fluffy yarn from Colinette; the latest Alpaca Silk, Cashmere and Merino yarn from the Debbie Bliss collection.

Knitwear is being shown in all the latest designer collections and some versions of designer garments have been included in simplified form to make them easy to knit – the results are chic and professional looking. These patterns will help you practise your techniques and will lead you on to more advanced knitting. Two of the designers who have contributed projects, Vikki Haffenden and Jane Rota, both work in the Fashion and Textile Department of Brighton University in the UK. Their expertise in knitwear fashion and their street-level understanding of what fashion students are wearing have helped them produce some of the really fantastic garments.

The mobile-phone cover (see page 74) was suggested by the author's teenage daughter, Maddy. She and her friends loved the idea of having something individual and fun in which to carry their phones. After all, mobile phones are generally pretty grey and boring for a colour-loving teenager; it's a pity that corporate grey cars can't be given the same treatment!

The dog jackets (see page 87) were an inspiration from Roger Perkins, an avid dog lover who can always be relied on for an original and amusing idea. Why dress your dog in a boring plastic jacket when the 'must haves' this season in the doggy world of fashion are shark fins and pom-poms?

There are also two sewing projects, still with knitting in mind. Just as an apprentice metalworker or gunsmith used to make the tools he would need for his craft, we've put together projects for a yarn tote bag (see page 94) and a needle case using fake cow fur (see page 96) .

Other projects demonstrate how individual yarn qualities, as well as accessories and textures, can turn a plain knitted garment into something individual and special. The designer of the chunky tasselled scarf (see page 78) fell in love with the hand-dyed yarn, designed a simple, basic scarf and turned it into a crowd stopper. Also included in the patterns that follow are pom-poms (see page 84–87), tassels (see page 85), and knitted flowers (see page 82). The current trend for ribbons, buttons and beads has also been an inspiration, so start rummaging in your local charity shops

or in your nearest haberdashery shop to find vintage or interesting ones. The design of the button handbag with its ribbon and buttons (see page 86) is, literally, straight from the catwalk and because it has no shaping, it's a delight to knit. The patterns are designed to be adaptable so you can easily change the accessories and styling to personalise your item.

There are plenty of designs that are ideal first projects. The easy jumper (see page 56) is just what it says: a cosy style that's a joy to wear. The scarves, hats and bags are also perfect items to practise simple stitching techniques. The pattern for the motif on the mobile phone cover (see page 74) uses the Fairisle technique (see pages 38–39) and the motif on the Dare-to-wear bikini (see page 72) uses the intarsia technique. The make-up bag (see page 82) is a

glamorous little number giving you the chance to have a go at some beading.

Don't be put off by abbreviations as they are all explained opposite. And if you drop a stitch, just turn to pages 40–41 for guidance. Refer, also, to the list of stockists on page 99.

Remember: every great garment begins with a first stitch and the making is as much fun as the wearing.

  Patterns...Funky Fashions

Abbreviations

alt	alternate		p2tog	purl two stitches together
beg	begin(ning)		r	row
bo	bind off (cast off)		rem	remaining
cm	centimetre		rep	repeat
cn	cable needle		rept	repeat
co	cast on		rs	right side
cont	continue		rev st st	reverse stocking stitch
dec	decrease		sk	skip
dk	double knitting		skpo	slip one, knit one, pass slipped stitch over
dpn	double pointed needle		sl	slip
foll	following		sl l	slip one
fwd	forward		Ssk	slip one knitwise, slip one knitwise, knit two together putting left hand needle into the front of the right hand needle's stitches.
g st	garter stitch			
in; ins	inches			
inc	increase		Ssp	slip one knitwise, slip one knitwise, return to left hand needle and purl two together upwards through back of sts
incl	including			
K	knit			
k1	knit one		st	stitch
K2tog	knit two stitches together		sts	stitches
m1	make one		st st	stocking stitch
mb	make bobble		tbl	through back of loop
mm	millimetre		tog	together
no	number		ws	wrong side
oz	ounce		wyb	with yarn in back
patt	pattern		wyf	with yarn in front
P	purl		yb	yarn back
p1	purl one		yf	yarn forward
pb	place bead		yfwd	yarn forward
pfb	purl into the front and the back of the stitch		yon	yarn over needle
pnso	pass next stitch over		yrn	yarn round needle
psso	pass slipped stitch over			
ptbl	purl through back loop			

The easy jumper

This oversize unisex sweater is amazingly quick to knit in garter stitch. The yarn is really luxurious – as I was knitting it my thoughts wandered from atmospheric views of Paris and the Seine and fashion catwalks to the tempting sights and smells of croissants, coffee and champagne.

EQUIPMENT
1 pair 8mm needles
1 darning needle

YARN
10–11 x 100g balls Rowan Polar Wool, shade 645 Winter White

TENSION
Using 8mm needles with stocking stitch 12 sts x 16 rows = 10cm (4in) square.
Using 8mm needles with garter stitch 12 sts x 20 rows = 10cm (4in) square.

SIZING
To fit chest sizes: 92/97/102cm (36/38/40in)
Final knitted size: 112/117/122cm (44/46/48in)

METHOD
Back
Cast on 68/70/72 sts.

Row 1: Knit 1 row into back of stitch.
Row 2: Purl 1 row.
Row 3: Knit 1 row.
Row 4: Purl 1 row.
Row 5: Knit 1 row.
Row 6: Purl 1 row.
These 6 rows form the curled edging.
Knit 70/71/72 rows or until work measures 37/37.5/38cm (14^1/$_2$/14^3/$_4$/15in).
(just knit and no purl for garter stitch)

Decrease 2 sts at beginning of the next 2 rows.
Knit 71/72/73 rows or until work measures 68.5/69/69.5cm (27/27^1/$_4$/27^1/$_2$in).
Cast off.

Front
Cast on 68/70/72 sts.
Knit 1 row into back of stitch.
Knit 5 rows stocking stitch.

Knit 70/71/72 rows or until work measures 37/37.5/38cm (14^1/$_2$/14^3/$_4$/15in).
Decrease 2 sts at beginning of next 2 rows.
Knit 16 rows.
Knit 32/33/34 turn. Slip remaining stitches on to a spare needle.
Knit 32/33/34 sts.
Knit 32/33/34 sts and turn.
K2tog and continue to end.
Continue knitting like this and K2tog at the neck edge at beginning of every 4th row until work measures 68.5/69/69.5cm (27/27^1/$_4$/27^1/$_2$in).
Cast off.
Return to the stitches held on the spare needle and knit from the neck edge, rejoining yarn.
Knit 32/33/34 sts.
Knit 32/33/34 sts.
K2tog and continue to end of row.
Continue knitting like this and k2tog at the neck edge at beginning of every 4th row until work measures 68.5/69/69.5cm (27/27^1/$_4$/27^1/$_2$in).
Cast off.

Sleeves
Cast on 31/33/35 sts.
Knit 1 row into back of stitch.
Knit 5 rows stocking stitch.
Knit 84 rows or until work measures 43cm (17in),

increasing 1 stitch at each end of every 4 rows.
Cast off.

Making up

Join shoulder seams.

Join sleeves to the main body of the garment.

Join side seams.

Join sleeve seams.

Sew in any ends.

Steam garment to shape gently.

Adding the neck trim

1. With the right side facing you and beginning at a shoulder, pick up and knit 21 (don't worry if you have 1 or 2 extra or 1 or 2 fewer stitches, but do keep looking at the stitches you are picking up to check they look fairly neat).

2. Knit 5 rows of stocking stitch and cast off.

3. Repeat for the other side of the neck edge.

4. Then pick up and knit 22 sts across the back neck. Knit 5 rows stocking stitch and cast off.

5. Join the edges of the neck trim and sew in the ends.

Unisex hoody

This hoody is a 'cuddle up' cosy affair, ideal for wearing outside for bonfire nights or summer barbecues when the temperature drops. The textural edging gives it a special quality and updates the standard rib border with a 4 x 4 rib that is alternated into a chunky basketweave over 12 rows. One of the rewards of chunky knitting is that it grows fast! If you'd rather not do the basketweave, substitute a plain 4 x 4 rib to cover these 12 rows. You can go quite wild or be subtle and gentle with the colours on this one. If you use an individual design based on your three favourite colours, no one else will ever turn up in the same hoody!

EQUIPMENT

1 pair 6.5mm needles
1 circular 6.5mm needle (for hood)
2 x stitch holders
A row counter (optional)

YARN

Yarn A: Debbie Bliss Merino Chunky, shade 612 Dark Plum
Yarn B: Debbie Bliss Merino Chunky, shade 205 Teal
Yarn C: Debbie Bliss Merino Chunky, shade 700 Scarlet
Most chunky yarns that knit to this tension can be substituted.

SIZES

Small sizes are given in the instructions with medium, large and Xlarge in brackets.

	SMALL UK 8–10	MEDIUM UK 12–14	LARGE UK 16–18	XLARGE UK 18–20
Bust:	81–86cm	91–97cm	102–108cm	110–115cm
	(32–34in)	(36–38in)	(40–42$^{1}/_{2}$in)	(43–45in)
Finished	96cm	108cm	114cm	120cm
bust	(37$^{5}/_{4}$in)	(42$^{1}/_{2}$in)	(44$^{5}/_{4}$in)	(47in)
Finished	58cm	60cm	62cm	64cm
length:	(23in)	(23$^{1}/_{2}$in)	(24$^{1}/_{2}$in)	(25in)

YARN

(number of 50g/1oz balls)

	SMALL UK 8–10	MEDIUM UK 12–14	LARGE UK 16–18	XLARGE UK 18–20
A Main:	12	13	14	15
B Contrast:	8	9	9	10
C Stripe:	1	1	1	1

TENSION

Using 6.5mm needles with stocking stitch 14 sts x 19 rows = 10cm (4in) square.

METHOD

Back

In yarn B on straight needles cast on 68 [76/80/84] sts.

Next row: K1 row.

Next row: Change to yarn A. *K4, P4 and rep from * until 4 sts from end, K4.

(Note: in the large size, there will not be the odd 4 sts to k or p at the end, and consequently the following row will read 'K4, P4 to end').

Next row: *P4, K4, rep from * until 4 sts from end, P4.

Rep these previous 2 rows so there are 4 rows in total. You have now finished your first basketweave square.

Next row: *P4, K4, rep from * until 4 sts from end, P4.

(Note: in the large size, there will not be the odd 4 sts to K or P at the end, and consequently the following row will read 'P4, K4 to end').

Next row: *K4, P4 rep from * until 4 sts from end, K4.

Rep these 2 rows so there are 4 rows in total. You have now finished your second basketweave square.

Rep the first basketweave square once more.

Next row: K1 row.

Starting with a knit row, work until your knitting measures 22cm [23/24/25cm] (8^1/$_2$in [9/9^1/$_2$/10in]) from the bottom edge. Make sure you end with a purl row.

Change to yarn C.

K2 rows.

Change to yarn B.

Work 20 rows in stocking stitch (starting with a knit row).

Change to yarn C.

K2 rows.

Change to yarn A.

Work 2 rows stocking stitch.

This brings you to the armhole shaping, which goes as follows:

Working in stocking stitch, cast off 3 [3/4/4] sts at beginning of next 2 rows.

Work 8 rows, decreasing 1 stitch at each end of the knit rows. (If you can do this 1 stitch in from the edge, it makes sewing up easier and neater.) See method at end.

After the last purl row there should be 52 [62/64/68] sts left on needle.

Work in stocking stitch until your knitting measures 21cm [23/23.5/24cm] (8^1/$_4$in [9/9^1/$_4$/9^1/$_2$in]) from the underarm cast off. Make sure you end with a knit row.

The shoulder and neck shaping (first side) goes as follows:

Next row: P21 [26/27/29] sts, place remaining 31 [36/37/39] sts on a stitch holder (these will be the back neck and the other shoulder).

Next row: Cast off 7 [7/8/8] sts (this is on the neck edge) at beginning of row, K to end.

Next row: Cast off 6 [7/7/7] sts at beginning of the row, P to end.

Next row: K1 row.

Next row: Cast off 5 [6/8/8] sts, P to end.

Final row: Cast off remaining sts and break yarn.

The shoulder and neck shaping (second side) goes as follows:

Take 21 [26/28/29] sts at the edge of the knitting off the stitch holder on to a needle, leaving the middle 10 on the holder and knit the left-hand shoulder.

Start with the wrong (purl) side facing you (you may need to shuffle sts from needle to needle to do this, but it makes it easier to knit).

Take a new end of yarn.

Row 1: P1 row.

Next row: Cast off 7 [7/7/8] sts at beginning of row, K to end.

Next row: Cast off 6 [7/8/8] sts at beginning of row, this is on the neck edge, P to end.

Next row: Cast off 5 [6/8/8] sts, K to end.

Final row: Cast off remaining sts, break yarn.

Leave middle sts on a stitch holder until the hood is knitted.

Front

Knit as the back until after the armhole shaping and there are 52 [62/66/68] sts left on the needle and your knitting measures 14.5cm [15.5/16/16.5cm] (5³/₄in [6/6¹/₄/6¹/₂in]) from the underarm cast off. Make sure you end with a knit row.

For the first neck shaping:

Next row: P21 [26/28/29] sts and place remaining 31 [36/38/39] sts on to a stitch holder.

Next row: Cast off 3 [4/4/5] sts at beginning of the row (this should be on the neck edge K to end).

Next row: P1 row.

Next row: Cast off 2 [2/2/2] sts at beginning of the row, K to end.

Next row: P1 row.

Work straight stocking stitch for 6 rows.

Next row: Decrease 1 [1/1/1] st at beginning of row and K to end.

The shoulder shaping comes in at the outside edge:

Next row: Cast off 6 [7/7/8] sts at beginning of row, P to end.

Next row: K1 row.

Next row: Cast off 5 [6/8/8] sts at beginning of row, P to end.

Next row: K1 row.

Row 1: Cast off remaining sts and break yarn.

For second neck shaping:

Take 21 [26/28/29] sts at the edge of the knitting off the holder on to a needle, leaving the middle 10 on the holder. Start with the wrong (purl) side facing you.

Take a new end of yarn.

Row 1: P1 row.

Next row: K1 row.

Next row: Cast off 3 [4/4/5] sts at beginning of row (this should be on the neck edge) K to end.

Next row: P1 row.

Next row: Cast off 2 [2/2/2] sts at beginning of row, K to end.

Next row: P1 row.

Work straight stocking stitch for 6 rows.

Next row: Decrease 1 [1/1/1] st at beginning of row and K to end.

Now the shoulder shaping comes in at the outside edge:

Next row: Cast off 6 [7/7/8] sts at beginning of row, P to end.

Next row: K1 row.

Next row: Cast off 5 [6/8/8] sts at beginning of row, P to end.

Next row: K1 row.

Final row: Cast off remaining sts and break yarn.

Sleeves (both worked the same)

In yarn B on straight needles cast on 36 [36/38/38] sts.

Row 1: K1 row.

Change to yarn A.

Knit same pattern as for basketweave as on back, increasing 1 st each end on rows 4, 8 and 12. (For the two larger sizes, if you want the basketweave to match at the seams, you will need to start the pattern with P1 and then continue the *K4, P4* rep to the end where there will be K4, P2 to finish.)

K1 row.

Starting with a knit row, knit in stocking stitch, increasing 1 st each end of the 2nd [7th/0th/4th] row and every following 5th [5th/6th/5th] row until your knitting measures 35cm [37.5/39/40cm] (13³/₄in [14³/₄/15¹/₄/15³/₄in]) from cast on. Make sure you end with a purl row.

Throughout the following rows, continue increasing on every 5th [5th/6th/5th] row as before.

Change to yarn C.

K2 rows.

Change to yarn B.

K20 rows in stocking stitch. Stop increasing when there are 70 [72/74/76] sts on the needle.

Change to yarn C.

K2 rows.

Change to yarn A.

Work 2 rows in stocking stitch (starting with a K row).

Start the underarm shaping:

Next 2 rows: Cast off 4 sts at beginning of both.

Next 24 [24/26/26] rows, decrease 1 st at both ends of every knit row only.

Next 4 rows: Cast off 3 [4/4/5] sts at beginning of each row.

Next 2 rows: Cast off 5 [5/5/5] sts at beginning of each row.

Final row: Mark centre of remaining stitches and cast them off.

Hood

Sew up the shoulder seams.

In yarn A, with the circular needle, starting at the centre front, pick up 68 [72/78/82] sts evenly around the neck. Put a marker at the centre front.

Knit 2 rows completely round in a circle.

Next row: K4 [6/9/11] sts, inc 1st, *K6, inc 1st*, rep * to * until last 4 [6/9/11] sts, knit to end.

Change to yarn B.

Next 4 rows: continue to knit in a circle, purling 6 stitches on either side of the centre mark, so they are in reverse stocking stitch.

Next row: Turn the knitting at the centre mark and work back around the circle so there is a split at the centre front. Carry on with the reverse stocking stitch on the middle stitches as before.

Continue this, keeping the split in the centre front for 78 [78/80/80] rows or until the knitting measures 40cm [40/41/41cm] (15³⁄₄in [15³⁄₄/16/16in]) from neck edge.

Transfer the stitches equally to 2 needles, so the front of the hood is at the point of the needles and the right sides are facing.

Take a 3rd needle of roughly the same size.

To get a nice smooth join, cast off with the 'three-needle cast-off', as follows:

Put both filled needles together and hold exactly as you would normally hold the left-hand needle.

Take the 3rd needle in your right hand and insert it through the 1st stitch on both needles in a knitwise manner.

Knit both stitches together.

Do the same again and then pull the 1st stitch you just made over the last one, as you would when casting off normally.

Carry on to the end repeating this process, and pulling the last stitch through.

Depending on your yarn, dry or wet block the pieces and sew up the side seams.

To decrease one stitch in from the edge at the beginning of a row gives a right-hand pointing slant to the stitch and is called the K2tog method:

On a knit row, K1 st, knit 2 together, K to end.

On a purl row, p1 st, purl 2 together and P to end.

To decrease one stitch in from the edge at the end of a row gives a left-hand pointing slant to the stitch and is called the Ssk or Slip, Slip, Knit method:

On a knit row, K to 3 sts from the end. Slip the next 2 sts one after the other knitwise off the left-hand needle. Then insert the left-hand needle up through the front of these sts from left to right. Bring your yarn through as usual and make a knit stitch.

On a purl row (Ssp or Slip, Slip, Purl) it is a little more complicated, so K to position and do the slipping as for a knit row, but then slip them back on to the left-hand needle and insert the right needle at the back up from below through both these stitches and purl them together.

Alpaca cardigan

This cardigan was inspired by the geometric filet-lace edgings often found on antique tablecloths. The moss stitch is knitted as you go along, creating a firm front border while also maintaining the garment's shape at the hip. The luxurious Alpaca Silk yarn (80 per cent Alpaca and 20 per cent silk) turns a simple cardigan into an exquisite, sensual experience. Accentuate this sensuous luxury by choosing a wide, softly flowing tonal ribbon as a decorative front fastening.

EQUIPMENT

1 pair 4.5mm needles.
Stitch holder
Row counter (optional)

YARN

Debbie Bliss Alpaca Silk, shade 25010 Coral

RIBBON

2m (2yd) of 4cm (1¹/₂in) wide soft satin ribbon in a tone of the main colour.

SIZES

Small sizes are given in the instructions with medium, large and Xlarge in brackets.

	SMALL UK 8–10	MEDIUM UK 12–14	LARGE UK 16–18	XLARGE UK 18–20
Bust:	81–86cm	91–97cm	102–108cm	110–115cm
	(32–34in)	(36–38in)	(40–42¹/₂in)	(43–45in)
Finished bust:	92cm	108cm	114cm	120cm
	(36in)	(42¹/₂in)	(44³/₄in)	(47in)
Finished length:	56cm	60cm	62cm	64cm
	(22in)	(23¹/₂in)	(24¹/₂in)	(25in)

YARN

(number of 50g/1oz balls)

	SMALL UK 8–10	MEDIUM UK 12–14	LARGE UK 16–18	XLARGE UK 18–20
	13	16	19	21

TENSION

Using 4.5mm needles with stocking stitch 18 sts x 23 rows = 10cm (4in) square.

METHOD

Note: If you can do your shaping at the sides of the pieces one stitch in from the edge, it will give a prettier finish and a neater edge to sew up. The shaping at the front neck edge is already positioned inside the moss stitch in the pattern.

Back

If you want to do a decorative decrease, use Ssk (see page 61) on beginning the decrease and K2tog on the end one.

Cast on 82 [96/104/110] sts.
Work moss stitch border as follows:
K1, P1, rep * to * to end.
P1, K1, rep * to * to end.
Repeat these 2 rows until there are 8 rows of knitting.

Work 2 rows stocking stitch, decreasing 1st each end on the 2nd row.
Work 20 rows of the main pattern, decreasing 1st each end every 10th row.
Work 10 rows of the main pattern increasing 1st each end on the 10th row.
In stocking stitch, carry on as follows:
Work 32 [36/38/42] rows, increasing 1st each end every 13 [16/17/18] rows.

Start of underarm shaping:

Cast off 3 [4/5/5] sts at beginning of next 2 rows.

Work 1 [1/3/6] rows, decreasing 1st each end.

Work 14 [16/16/12] rows, decreasing 1st at each underarm edge on every 2nd row.

Next row: Work straight in stocking stitch to row 116 [126/130/134] or until knitting measures 51cm [57/57.5/58.5cm] (20in [22$\frac{1}{2}$/22$\frac{1}{2}$/23in]) from cast-on edge.

Start of neck and shoulder shaping:

In this shaping the cast-offs are given a smoother line (instead of the traditional 'steps') by knitting 2 sts together at the end of the preceding row. This tip is borrowed from Elizabeth Zimmerman's *Knitting Without Tears*. It is described here, and it could also be applied to the front-panel shoulder shaping.

Next row: K27 [28/29/30] sts, put remaining sts on a holder, putting in a centre-back marker at middle of whole piece.

Next row: Turn knitting and cast off 4 [4/4/5] sts at neck edge, P to end.

Next row: K to end, knitting last 2 sts together.

Next row: Cast off 2 [3/4/3] sts at neck edge, P to end.

Next row: Cast off 4 [3/3/4] sts at shoulder edge and K to end, knitting last 2 sts together at neck edge.

Next row: Cast off 1 [0/0/0] sts at neck edge, P to end of row, purling last 2 sts together at shoulder edge.

Next row: Cast off 3 [3/4/3] sts at shoulder edge and K to end, knitting last 2 sts together at neck edge.

Next row: P to end, purling last 2 sts together at shoulder edge.

Next row: Cast off 4 [3/3/3] sts at shoulder edge and K to end.

Next row: P to end, purling last 2 sts together at shoulder edge.

Next row: Cast off remaining sts.

Front

Pattern A:

This is the basic pattern with the moss stitch integrated into the front panel.

*K to 4 sts from end, K1, P1, K1, P1.

P1, K1, P1, K1, P to end*. Rep * to *.

If you want to do decorative decreasing, it is worked as follows for the shaping on the sides of the body:

On a knit row: K1, decrease 1 st using Ssk method (see page 55), K to 4 sts from edge, K1, P1, K1, P1.

On a purl row: P1, K1, P1, K1, P to 3 sts from the edge and decrease 1 st by Ssp method (see page 55).

Decrease B:

The decreasing for the V-neck worked inside the moss stitch is as follows:

On a knit row: K to 6 stitches from end, decrease 1 stitch (K2tog), K1, P1, K1, P1.

On a purl row: P1, K1, P1, K1, decrease 1st (P2tog), P to end.

Left-hand side:
Cast on 40 [48/52/54] sts and knit moss stitch as back for 8 rows:
Row 1: *K1, P1*, rep * to *.
Next row: *P1, K1*, rep * to *.

Work 2 rows main pattern, decreasing 1st at the side edge on row 2.
Work 20 [20/24/20] rows of the main pattern, decreasing 1st at the side edge every 10 [10/8/10] rows.
Work 10 [10/6/10] rows of the main pattern, increasing 1st at the side edge at row 10 [10/6/10].

Start of front V shaping:
Next row: Work 1 row as decrease B (this will be a decrease on the front edge, inside the moss stitch border).
Work 18 [18/38/42] rows of the main pattern decreasing as decrease B, inside the moss stitch every 6 [6/7/6] rows, and increasing on the side edge every 9 [15/11/17] rows.
Note: For large size only, knit 3 rows straight and skip the next instruction, going straight to the underarm shaping.

Work 14 [18/0/0] rows of the main pattern decreasing as decrease B, inside the moss stitch every 6 [7/0/0] rows, and increasing on the side edge every 9 [15/0/0] rows.

Start of underarm shaping:
Continue with the front decreases at every 7 [7/7/6] rows to the end of the panel, but cast off 3 [3/5/5] sts on the side edge for the underarm on the next knit row.
Work 1 [1/3/6] rows, decreasing 1st every other row at the underarm edge.
Work 14 [16/18/12] rows, decreasing 1st at the underarm edge on every 2nd row.
Next row: Continuing the front decreasing, knit straight up on the armhole side edge for 34 [36/36/38] rows. This will bring you to the shoulder.

Start the shoulder shaping:
Still working in main pattern A, cast off 4 [4/4/5] sts on the shoulder edge on the next knit row.

Next row: P1 row pattern A.
Next row: Cast off 4 [5/5/5] sts on the shoulder edge.
Next row: P1 row pattern A.
Next row: Cast off 5 [5/5/5] sts on the shoulder edge.
Next row: P1 row pattern A.
Next row: Cast off remaining sts.
Right-hand side:
Pattern A:
This is the basic pattern with the moss stitch integrated into the front panel.
*K to 4 sts from end, K1, P1, K1, P1.
P1, K1, P1, K1, P to end*. Rep * to *.

If you want to do decorative decreasing, it is worked as follows for the shaping on the sides of the body:
On a knit row: P1, K1, P1, K1, K to 3 sts from end, decrease 1 stitch (K2tog).
On a purl row: P1, decrease 1st (P2tog), P to 4 sts from end, K1, P1, K1, P1.

Decrease B:
The decreasing for the V-neck worked inside the moss stitch is as follows:
On a knit row: P1, K1, P1, K1, decrease 1st (Ssk, see page 61), K to end.
On a purl row: P to 6 sts from end, decrease 1 stitch (Ssp, see page 61), K1, P1, K1, P1.

Right-hand side:
Cast on 40 [48/52/54] and knit moss stitch as back for 8 rows:
Row 1: *K1, P1*, rep * to *.
Next row: *P1, K1*, rep * to *.

Work 2 [2/2/2] rows main pattern, decreasing 1st at the side edge every 2 [2/2/2] rows.
Work 20 [20/24/20] rows of the main pattern, decreasing 1st at the side edge every 10 [10/8/10] rows.
Work 10 [10/6/10] rows of the main pattern, increasing 1st at the side edge at row 10 [10/6/10].

Start of front V shaping:

Next row: Work 1 row as decrease B (this will be a decrease on the front edge, inside the moss-stitch border).

Work 18 [18/38/42] rows of the main pattern decreasing as decrease B, inside the moss stitch every 6 [6/7/6] rows, and increasing on the side edge every 9 [15/11/17] rows.

Note: For large size only, knit 3 rows straight and skip the next instruction, going straight to the underarm shaping.

Work 14 [18/0/0] rows of the main pattern decreasing as decrease B, inside the moss stitch every 6 [7/0/0] rows, and increasing on the side edge every 9 [15/0/0] rows.

Start of underarm shaping:

Continue with the front decreases at every 7 [7/7/6] rows to the end of the panel, but cast off 3 [3/5/5] sts on the side edge for the underarm on the next knit row.

Work 1 [1/3/6] rows, decreasing 1st every other row at the underarm edge.

Work 14 [16/18/12] rows, decreasing 1st at the underarm edge on every 2nd row.

Next row: Continuing the front decreasing, knit straight up on the armhole side edge for 34 [36/36/38] rows. This will bring you to the shoulder.

Start the shoulder shaping:

Working in main pattern A, cast off 4 [4/4/5] sts on the shoulder edge on the next knit row.

Next row: P1 row pattern A.

Next row: Cast off 4 [5/5/5] sts on the shoulder edge.

Next row: P1 row pattern A.

Next row: Cast off 5 [5/5/5] sts on the shoulder edge.

Next row: P1 row pattern A.

Next row: Cast off remaining sts.

Sleeves

(Both are the same.)

Cast on 42 [46/48/50] sts and knit moss stitch as for back.

Continue in stocking stitch as follows starting with a K row:

Next row: Increase 1st at each end of row.

Next section: Work 91 [93/30/72] rows in stocking stitch, increasing 1st at each edge every 8 [7/6/6] rows.

Next section: Work 0 [0/63/23] rows in stocking stitch, increasing 1st at each edge every 0 [0/7/7] rows until your work measures 43.5cm [45/45/45cm] (17in [18/18/18in]) from the cast-on edge. Finish on a P row.

Next row: Cast off 4 [3/3/4] sts at beginning of row, K to end.

Next row: Cast off 4 [3/3/4] sts at beginning of row, P to end.

Next row: Work 4 [7/8/7] rows stocking stitch, decreasing 1st at each end of every row.

Next row: Work 6 [9/12/4] rows stocking stitch, decreasing 1st at each end of every 3 [3/3/4] rows.

Next row: Work 18 [12/10/7] rows stocking stitch, decreasing 1st at each end of every 2 [2/2/3] rows.

Next row: Work 1 [7/7/7] rows stocking stitch, decreasing 1st each at end of every 1 [1/1/1] rows.

Next row: Cast off remaining sts marking centre of sleeve head. 20 [22/24/26]. Row 134 [138/140/142].

Making up

1. Block out carefully as the moss stitch has a tendency to curl – in fact, the whole garment will benefit from this. To make everything easier while sewing up, line up the decreases as you do this.

2. Do all the sewing in the yarn in which the garment is knitted. Join the shoulder seams, matching moss stitch patterns and preferably using mattress stitch (see page 45).

3. Set in the sleeves, matching the centre sleeve head to the shoulder seam and easing in any fullness. Sew up with mattress stitch.

4. Join the side seams and the underarm seams with mattress stitch. Take care to match up the decreases to give a professional finish.

5. Finally, sew in ends and sew on the ribbons, positioning them at the bottom of the front decreases.

Fingerless gloves

These cute and cosy gloves have a little 'ticket to ride' pocket on the front and are very simple to make. If you can cast on and off, rib and do simple increases, you will have no problems knitting these.

EQUIPMENT
1 pair 4.5mm needles
1 pair 5mm needles

YARN
Yarn A: 1 x 50g ball Debbie Bliss Cashmerino Aran, shade 502 Pea Green
Yarn B: 1 x 50g ball Debbie Bliss Cashmerino Aran, shade 505 Yellow
Yarn C: 1 x 50g ball Debbie Bliss Cashmerino Aran, shade 609 Burnt Orange

TENSION
Using 5mm needles 18sts x 24 rows = 10cm (4in) square.

METHOD
With the 4.5mm needles and yarn B, cast on 36 stitches using the two-strand thumb method by preference, but any method will do.

The two-strand thumb method
This technique that uses the thumb as another needle makes a firm but elastic cast on that's good for rib edges.
Leaving a tail of yarn 3 times as long as the proposed wrist circumference, cast on, make a slip knot and slip it over the right-hand needle.
1. Hold the needle in your right hand and the tail of yarn in your left hand, so it is gripped underneath your turned-under fingers, leaving a strand of approximately 10cm (4in) stretching from your left hand towards the right-hand needle.
2. Lay your thumb over the top of this strand and draw an anti-clockwise circle with the end of your thumb so the

yarn is wrapped clockwise neatly around it.
3. Next slide the tip of the right-hand needle up under the front loop on your thumb, and pass the right-hand yarn over from the back between thumb and needle, as if making a knit stitch.
4. Slip the loop off your left thumb as if completing the knit stitch; pull the tails to tighten the stitch and repeat for as many stitches as you need to cast on.

While knitting these gloves, keep checking the size against your hand; if they need adjusting in length, do half the extra rows in the plain section after the increasing for the thumb and the rest in the straight section after the thumb hole.

Right-hand glove
Work 18 rows in K1, P1 rib to create the wrist rib.
Change to 5mm needles and yarn A.
Work 2 rows stocking stitch.
**Then continue in stocking stitch as follows: *increase 1 st on third-from-last st at the end of the next row by knitting into front and back* (see increase instructions on page 33), (37 sts on needle).
P1 row*.
Rept * to * until there are 42 sts on the needle.
You've now finished the right thumb shaping.
Work 14 rows in stocking stitch.

Creating the thumb hole:
Cast off 14 sts at the end of the row and cut your yarn, leaving a tail.
On the empty needle, with new yarn, cast on 10 sts, bring the yarn to the front, and continue to purl the stitches on the other needle, knitting the tail with the new yarn for a few stitches to catch it in (38 sts on needle).**
Work 2 rows in stocking stitch.
Change to yarn B.
Work 4 rows in stocking stitch.
Change to 4.5mm needles.

Patterns...Funky Fashions

Work 4 rows in K1, P1 rib.

Cast off as normal on the knit stitches but where there is a purl stitch, take the yarn back when you slip the second stitch over the first stitch and bring it back again if you want to purl the next stitch.

Left–hand glove

Knit as right-hand glove, swapping the shaping instructions ** to ** to the opposite side and then continuing to the end as with the right glove.

Cast off.

The 'ticket to ride' pocket

Using 4.5mm needles and yarn C, and starting from about the 6th stitch in from the thumb–hole edge, pick up 9 sts along the 10th row up from the end of the wrist rib. (To do this, have the right side facing and one needle in your right hand, then push the needle from front to back through the centre of the existing stitch. Wind the yarn round the needle in a knit action and draw the loop through to create a new stitch on the needle). When you finish this row, the yarn will be on the wrong side of the knitting, so break it and start with a fresh end. You can vary the position depending on the size of pocket you want.

Break your yarn (it is on the wrong side of the fabric).

K1 row into the back of the stitches.

P1 row.

Work another 8 rows in stocking stitch.

Cast off.

Pocket flap

This has a bit of increasing and decreasing to shape the edges with a left and right slant. It's rather pretty, but if it's not your thing, just knit the flap straight for 6 rows, cast off and add a loop as described. You can try shaping another time!

Find the row that is 2 rows above the cast off of the pocket edge and using yarn A, pick up through 11 sts, as you did with the pocket, starting from 1 st outside the width of the

pocket and ending one st outside the other end.

K1 row into the back of the stitches.

P1 row.

Work another 6 rows stocking stitch, decreasing 1 st each end until 3 sts are left on the needle.

If you use the Ssk method (see page 61) on the first decrease in the row it looks better. On a knit row, slip 1 knitwise twice, insert left needle into front of these 2 sts from the left and K2tog; on a purl row, slip one knitwise twice, return these 2 sts to left needle, insert right needle from back upwards through second.

Cast off.

With a crochet hook, chain a button loop on the pocket flap.

Sew up the thumb seam with mattress stitch, using the ends of the yarns where possible and matching the colour to that of the stripe you are joining.

Sew in any odd ends.

Mark where the joins between the fingers occur, and sew or crochet a chain across with yellow yarn.

Finally, add the button of your choice to the pocket flap.

Poncho

Although this poncho looks luxurious and weighty, it is in fact very light – and incredibly warm. The mixing of the different quality yarns adds visual texture. If you don't want to wear it as a poncho, why not just decadently wrap it around your neck and shoulders – and create a snug cocoon for yourself?

EQUIPMENT

1 pair 20mm needles

YARN

3 x 100g balls Rowan Biggy Print, shade 237 Tickle
1 x 50g ball Rowan Handknit Cotton, shade 313 Slick

METHOD

Using the chunky (Rowan Biggy Print) yarn, cast on 20 sts.
Knit 4 rows of stocking stitch and break off the yarn.
Change to the finer Handknit Cotton yarn and knit 4 rows of stocking stitch and break off the yarn.
Change to the chunky (Rowan Biggy Print) yarn and knit 4 rows of stocking stitch.
Continue with these yarn stripes in blocks of 4 rows until you have 28 rows or 7 bands of chunky (Rowan Biggy Print) stripes.
Cast off.

Knit a second identical piece.

1   Join the 2 pieces together, leaving a central opening of approximately 25cm (10in) for the head.
2   To add the fringe, cut about 100 x 25cm (10in) lengths of Rowan Biggy Print yarn.
3   Place them around the edge of the poncho, deciding on the space intervals (5–6cm/2–2¹/₂in seems about right). Then attach the fringe.

Cotton summer hat

Using cotton for this item makes a comfortably soft but easily reshaped hat for the beach or any hot summer's day. You can pack it tightly in a bag or pocket, give it a quick shake and it's ready to go. Play your own colour games and have fun with the stripes to match your wardrobe. Choose a bright and sassy version or a subtle and laid-back interpretation – it's up to you!

EQUIPMENT
1 pair 3.75mm needles
Row counter (optional)

YARN
1 x 50g ball Rowan Handknit Cotton in each of the following 3 colours:
Yarn A: shade 318 Seafarer
Yarn B: shade 320 Buttercup
Yarn C: shade 319 Mango Fool

SIZING
A hat with a 55–58cm (21^1/$_2$–23in) head circumference like this one should fit most head measurements.

TENSION
Using 3.75mm needles with stocking stitch 20 sts x 30 rows = 10cm (4in) square.

ABBREVIATIONS
yfwd (yarn forward)
sl1 (slip 1)
ybk (yarn back)
Ssk or the Slip, Slip, Knit method. On a knit row, when you get to where the decrease is required, slip the next 2 sts one after the other knitwise off the left-hand needle on to the right hand one. Then insert the left-hand needle up through the front of these sts from left to right. Bring your yarn through as usual and make a knit stitch.

Ssp or the Slip, Slip, Purl method: On a purl row, when you get to where the decrease is required, slip the next 2 sts one after the other knitwise off the left-hand needle on to the right hand one. Then slip them back on to the left hand needle. Insert the right needle at the back upwards from below through both these stitches and purl them together.

METHOD
With yarn A, cast on 115 sts.
Work 8 rows stocking stitch ending with a P row.
Change to yarn C, K2 rows garter stitch.
Change to yarn B, K8 rows stocking stitch, starting with a K row.
Change to yarn A.
Work 30 rows in linen stitch as follows:
Row 1: *K1, yfwd, sl1 purlwise, ybk. Rep from * to last stitch, K1.
Row 2: P1, *P1, ybk, sl1 purlwise, yfwd. Rep from * to last 2 sts, P2.

The linen stitch reduces stretch in the band so it gently grips the head while adding textural interest.

K1 row, increasing 1st at end of the row.

Work 7 rows in stocking stitch, increasing 1 st at each end of first row (118 sts).

Change to yarn B, work 7 rows stocking stitch, ending with a P row.

Change to yarn C, work 5 rows in garter stitch. On the 6th row, at every 4th stitch before making the stitch, reach down with the needle tip and catch the top loop of the last stitch in yarn B that is directly below the current stitch and make the new stitch through both loops. This pulls the knitting into a ripple and makes the rim of the crown.

Change to yarn A and K1 row, putting markers after the 13th stitch and between the following 4 blocks of 23 stitches (there should be another 13 left at the end).

For the crown shaping:

Work from now on in stocking stitch, starting with a P row.

Next row: *P1 row, decreasing first both sides of the markers. In each pair, first decrease should be P2tog, 2nd should be Ssp method (see above).

Next row: K1 row.

Next row: P1 row.

Next row: K1 row, decreasing first both sides of the markers. In each pair, first decrease should be Ssk method (see above), 2nd should be K2tog method.

Next row: P1 row.

Next row: K1 row, decreasing first both sides of the markers. In each pair, first decrease should be Ssk method (see above), 2nd should be K2tog method.

Next row: P1 row.

Next row: K1 row.

Next row: P1 row, decreasing first both sides of the markers. In each pair, first decrease should be P2tog, 2nd should be Ssp method (see above).

Next row: K1 row*.

Next 10 rows: Rep * to *.

Next row: P1 row.

Next row: K1 row, decreasing first both sides of the markers. In each pair, first decrease should be Ssk method (see

above), 2nd should be K2tog method.

Next 2 rows: P1 row.

Next row: K1 row, decreasing first both sides of the markers. In each pair, first decrease should be Ssk method (see above), 2nd should be K2tog method.

Next row: Thread yarn through the remaining 6 sts at the apex of the decreases.

Sew up the seam, matching yarn colours, draw last 6 sts into a point and sew in the ends securely.

Block over a tubular shape that will help the hat form a nice fit.

Dare-to-wear bikini

This natty bikini can compete confidently with the very latest beach fashions. The top could also be worn with shorts for a more sporty look. There is no doubt that this bikini is minimal and 'dare to wear', so pull both elements tight to fit snugly! The bikini is available in two sizes, small and medium, with the small size given first and the medium size following in brackets.

EQUIPMENT
1 pair 4mm needles
1 pair 3mm needles

YARN
1 x 50g balls Rowan Handknit DK Cotton, shade 309 Celery (edging)
2 x 50g ball Rowan Handknit DK Cotton, shade 313 Slick (main colour)
1 x 50g ball Rowan Handknit DK Cotton, shade 319 Mango Fool (flower)

TENSION
Using 4mm needles 20 sts x 28 rows = 10cm (4in) square.

ABBREVIATIONS
K2tog (knit 2 stitches together)
K2tog tbl (knit 2 stitches together through back loop)

METHOD
Top
Row 1: Using 4mm needles and the edging colour, cast on 35 [39] sts.
Row 2: Change to main colour.
Row 3: Knit 1 row into the back of the stitch.
Row 4: Purl 1 row.
Row 5: On the next row begin to knit the flower image after knitting 6 sts in the main colour. Copy the pattern from the chart shown here, while following the shaping instructions given below.

Shaping 1: K15 [17], K2tog tbl, K1, K2tog, K15 [17].
Shaping 2: Purl 1 row.
Shaping 3: K14 [16], K2tog tbl, K1, K2tog, K14 [16].
Shaping 4: Purl 1 row.
Shaping 5: Continue in this way, decreasing by a single stitch the number of stitches worked before K2tog tbl, K1, K2tog, and decrease by a single stitch the number of stitches knitted to the end of the row.

Next row: Purl 1 row.
Next row: Continue following these last 2 rows until 3 sts remain.
Next row: Purl 1 row.
Next row: Change to 3mm needles to knit cord for tie. Use main colour. Knit 3.

  Patterns...Funky Fashions

Next row: Slip these 3 sts back to needle in left hand.

Next row: Knit 3.

Next row: Continue in this way until the cord reaches approx. 29cm (11¹/₂in). Cast off.

Now add the trim. This will neaten the edge and allow you to add a highlight colour using 3mm needles and the main colour. With right side facing, pick up and knit up 1 side of top. Turn and knit back. Then cast off using the edging colour.

Next row: Repeat up the other side.

Next row: Pick up 3 sts at centre front of one side, knit in the same way as the cord for approximately 6cm (2¹/₂in). Cast off. Join to the other side's centre front. You may want to adjust this distance depending on your individual chest measurements.

Next row: Pick up 3 sts at one side of top, knit in the same way as the cord for approximately 50cm (19¹/₂in). Cast off. Repeat on the other side.

Pants

Row 1: Using 4mm needles and the edging colour, cast on 28 [32] sts.

Change to main yarn.

Row 2: Knit 1 row into back of stitch.

Row 3: Purl 1 row.

Row 4: On the next row begin to knit the flower image after knitting 6 sts in the main colour. Copy the pattern from the chart shown here, while following the shaping instructions given below.

Shaping 1: K2tog, knit to last 2 sts, K2tog.

Shaping 2: Purl.

Shaping 3: Continue in stocking stitch, decreasing 2 sts (as in shaping 1) every 5 rows until 14 sts remain.

Shaping 4: Continue in stocking stitch, decreasing 2 sts every 3 rows until 10 sts remain.

Shaping 5: Knit 4 rows.

Shaping 6: Increase 1 st, knit to last st, then increase 1 st.

Shaping 7: Continue in stocking stitch, increasing 2 st every 4 rows (as in shaping 6) until you have 22 sts.

Shaping 8: Continue in stocking stitch, increasing 2 sts every

3 rows until 50 [54] sts are on the needle.

Shaping 9: Using edging colour cast off.

Next row: Using 3mm needles and main colour, and with right side facing, pick up and knit around the leg edge of one side of the pants.

Next row: Knit.

Next row: Using edging colour, cast off.

Next 3 rows: Repeat previous 3 rows on the other side.

Next row: Using 3mm needles, and with right side facing, pick up and knit 3 sts at top the edge of the pants. Knit in the same way as the cord for approx. 32cm (12¹/₂in). Cast off.

Repeat the above sequence on the other top edges to form the ties for the pants.

Knit the flower image in intarsia (to avoid having any floats of yarn on the reverse).

Each colour block has its own ball of yarn, so make little wrappings of the colours you will need. Knit in stocking stitch, following the chart. When you change from one colour to another, twist one yarn around the other to link the colour blocks.

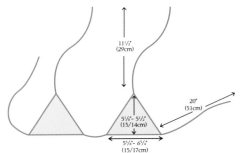

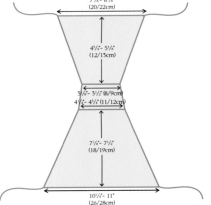

MOTIF

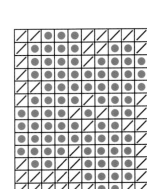

Mobile phone/iPod cover

This funky cover for a mobile phone, or for an iPod, is an ideal gift and a great excuse to show off your knitting skills. Use any combination of colours, and any double-knit yarn can be used for the main colour. In the motif pattern, Aran has been used for the motif in order to make the pink heart stand out, but any yarn can be used. Alternatively, as with the sock-yarn pattern, try using self-patterning sock yarn. There's no fiddling around with changing colours – you just knit from one ball of wool and use the size needles recommended for the yarn.

EQUIPMENT

1 pair 5mm needles (for motif cover)
1 pair 3.5mm needles (for sock-yarn cover)
Lining
1 snap fastener
1 button

YARN

Motif cover

Yarn A: 1 x 50g ball Rowan Wool Cotton, shade 946 Elf
Yarn B: 1 x 50g ball Debbie Bliss Cashmerino Aran, shade 616 Fuchsia

Sock-yarn cover

1 x 50g ball 6-ply Regia Sock Yarn, shade 5269 Las Vegas

TENSION

Using 5mm needles 22 sts x 24 rows = 10cm (4in) square (Wool Cotton).
Using 3.5mm needles 26 sts x 32 rows = 10cm (4in) square (Sock Yarn).

METHOD

Work in stocking stitch throughout (K x 1 row, P x 1 row).

Motif cover

1. Cast on 21 sts in yarn A.
2. Work 18 rows ending on a purl row.
3. Follow motif chart (A) using yarn A and B for next 13 rows, using the Fairisle technique (see page 38).
4. Work 20 rows in yarn A.
5. Follow motif chart (B) using yarn A and B for next 13 rows.
6. Work 22 rows in yarn A, ending with a purl row.
7. Decrease 1 st at each end of the next knit row and every following knit row until 11 sts remain.
8. Purl 1 row.
9. Cast off.

Sock-yarn cover

1. Cast on 21 sts.
2. Work 86 rows in stocking stitch, ending with a purl row.
3. Decrease 1 st at each end of the next knit row and every following knit row until 11 sts remain.
4. Purl 1 row.
5. Cast off.

Making up

Sew in ends.

Block and press.

Lining and finishing

1. Lay the knitted piece flat and measure a piece of lining
   fabric 1cm (¹/₃in) bigger than the knitted piece to allow
   for the seam. Lay the front face of the lining to the
   front face of the knitted piece and machine-sew 3 sides,
   leaving the top open. When you are stitching, leave the
   edges of the knitted stitches free so the sides can be
   sewn up later.

2. Turn the fabric inside out to reveal the right side of the
   knitted piece. At the top edge tuck the lining edge
   under and hand-stitch the rest of the lining to the
   knitted piece.

3. Fold so the right side is facing the right side and then
   bring the bottom edge of the fabric up to 1cm (¹/₃in)
   below the point where the decreasing starts and stitch
   the two side seams with the over-and-over method.
   Press the seams.

4. Sew a snap fastener on the inside of the flap and sew
   on a button as a decoration.

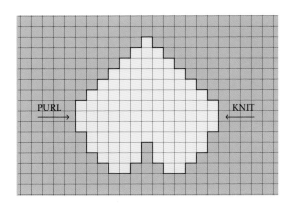

Chart A

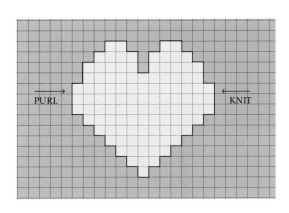

Chart B

Leg warmers

There is no need for leg warmers to be associated solely with the sporting and street fashions of the 1980s – they are now officially back on the streets in confident contemporary styles. This design, using a Cashmerino mix with Merino wool, provides the perfect comfort clothing for those cold winter days. This pattern can be used in combination with any chunky yarn.

EQUIPMENT
1 pair 7.5mm needles

YARN
2 x 100g balls Debbie Bliss Cashmerino Superchunky, shade 11 Red

TENSION
Using 7.5mm needles 12 sts x 17 rows = 10cm (4in) square.

METHOD
Knit both leg warmers in the same way.

Cast on 34 sts using 7.5mm needles.

Knit a 2-stitch rib as follows:
Row 1: K2 *P2, K2 rep from * to end.
Row 2: P2, *K2, P2, rep from * to end.

Continue these two rows until work measures 30.5cm (12in). Cast off in rib, making sure you take the yarn back when knitting and the yarn forward when purling your stitches.

Making up
Press each knitted piece (see page 46).
Sew up the seams.

Throw

This throw has an impressive selection of textures. The yarns have been chosen for their softness, so say goodbye to those annoying itchy blankets when you're curled up on the sofa. The throw is knitted in one piece, and on circular needles to hold the large amount of stitches. A neutral colourway has been chosen for this throw, but choose a colour combination that matches your own décor.

EQUIPMENT
1 pair circular 6mm needles 100cm (39¹/₄in) long
Stitch holder

YARN
Yarn A: 2 x 100g balls Rowan Ribbon Twist, shade 116 Riches

Yarn B: 4 x 50g balls Rowan Handknit Cotton, shade 253 Tope

Yarn C: 2 x 100g balls Rowan Polar, shade 645 Winter White

Yarn D: 2 x 50g balls Rowan Cotton Glacé, shade 730 Oyster (knit in a double thickness in combination with the Lurex Shimmer)

Yarn E: 1 x 25g ball Rowan Lurex Shimmer, shade 332 Antique White Gold (knit in a double thickness in combination with the Cotton Glacé)

Yarn F: 1 x 25g ball Rowan Lurex Shimmer, shade 330 Copper (knit in a double thickness in combination with the Cotton Glacé)

Yarn G: 3 x 100g hanks Debbie Bliss Maya, shade 07/062 (1¹/₂ ball for the main throw and 1¹/₂ ball for the edging)

Yarn H: 2 x 50g balls Debbie Bliss Alpaca Silk, shade 02 Cream

Yarn I: 1 x 100g hank Colinette Silkychic Tapis

METHOD
*Using a colour and yarn of your choice, knit 6 rows in garter stitch (knit).

Change colour and yarn. Knit 6 rows in stocking stitch (K1 row, P1 row)*.

Continue from * to * until throw measures 122.5cm (48in) or the required length.
Cast off.

For the edging:
Owing to the throw having a mixture of textures and yarn thicknesses, the edges will have an uneven quality. The throw will therefore be held together better with an edging.

1. Cast on 9 sts in yarn G.
2. Rows 1-2: *K1, P1* repeat *to* to end of row. This sets moss stitch. Repeat until work measures 5.1m (200in) or is at the required length.
3. Put the stitches on a stitch holder until you are certain that the edging is long enough for the throw, then cast off.
4. Sew the edging on the throw using the over-and-over method (see page 44).
5. Fold the edging to go round the corners of the throw. Then stitch the corners in place.

Tasselled garter stitch scarf and Garter stitch scarf

A scarf in garter stitch, the simplest of knitting structures using just knit stitch, is an ideal first project for beginners, particularly when in combination with chunky yarn and chunky needles. To give a touch of glamour, add some tassels to decorate the sides of the scarf. Any superchunky yarn can be used for this pattern, so choose your preferred yarn and colour and just start knitting.

EQUIPMENT

1 pair 12mm needles (with Colinette Point Five yarn)
1 pair 15mm needles (with Rowan Biggy Print yarn)

YARN

3 x 100g hanks Colinette Point Five, Blue Parrot
or
3 x 100g balls Rowan Biggy Print, shade 257 Choc Chip

TENSION

Colinette Point Five yarn: using 12mm needles 8 sts x 10 rows = 10cm (4in) square.
Rowan Biggy Print yarn: using 15mm needles 7.5 sts x 11.5 rows = 10cm (4in) square.

FINISHED SIZE

Length with Colinette Point Five yarn: 171cm (67in).
Length with Rowan Biggy Print yarn: 162cm (63½in).

  Patterns...Funky Fashions

TASSELLED SCARF

(using Point Five yarn)

With 12mm needles, cast on 12 sts.
Sl 1 st, K to end.
Repeat * to * until 2 hanks of yarn have been knitted,
leaving enough yarn to cast off.
Sew in ends.

To make the tassels, wrap the yarn twice around your hand
or a piece of card measuring approximately 8.5cm (3in) –
this makes a 4-strand tassel.
Attach the tassels on every other row along the bottom and
side ends (see fringe instructions on page 50).

GARTER STITCH SCARF

(using Rowan Biggy Print yarn)

With 15mm needles, cast on 8 sts.
Sl 1 st, K to end.
Repeat * to * until all 3 balls of yarn are used up, leaving just
enough yarn to cast off.
Sew in ends.

Tip: use a crochet hook to sew in the ends of superchunky
yarns. Alternatively, use a bodkin needle with a large
enough eye to thread superthick yarn.

Fluffy silky-chic scarf

This glamorous scarf wraps around the neck and ties at the front. The eyelash yarn is soft and silky and feels very luxurious.

EQUIPMENT

1 pair 6mm needles
Approximately 12 beads

YARN

1 x 100g hank Colinette Silkychic, shade Toscana

TENSION

Using 6mm needles 18 sts x 24 rows = 10cm (4in) square.

METHOD

Work in garter stitch (knit) throughout.

Cast on 1 st, leaving a 13.5cm (5in) tail.
Row 1: K1.
Row 2: Increase 1 st (2 sts).
Row 3: K2.
Row 4: Increase 1 st, inc 1 st (4 sts).
Row 5: Knit to end.
Row 6: Increase 1 st, knit to last st, inc 1 st (6 sts).

Repeat rows 5 and 6 until 16 sts remain on needle.
Knit straight until work measures 1.7m (67in).

Next row: K2tog, K to last st, K2tog.
Next row: Knit.
Repeat last 2 rows until 1 st remains.
Cast off, leaving a 20cm (8in) tail.

Make 2 tassels (see page 50), thread the tail with beads and stitch 1 tassel at each end of the scarf.

Beanie hat

All in all, this is just one evening's work. So, if the temperature drops, get home, dig out some fat needles and chunky yarn and by the morning you'll have made a warm hat – and an enviable fashion statement.

EQUIPMENT
1 pair 10mm needles

YARN
1 x 100g ball Rowan Big Wool, shade 001 White Hot (also shown in shade 014 Whoosh)

TENSION
Using size 10mm needles 8.5 sts x 13 rows = 10cm (4in) square.

METHOD
Knit in stocking stitch throughout.
Small size in first brackets, large size in square brackets.

Cast on 37 [45] sts.
Knit 18 [20] rows in stocking stitch.

Shaping the top:
Tip: Be sure to count the stitches at the end of each row when shaping.

Next row 1: With rs facing *K9, K2tog, rep from * to last st, K1 (33 [41] sts).
Next row 2: Work 1 row.
Next row 3: *K7, K3tog, rep from * to end (25 [33] sts).
Next row 4: Work 1 row.
Next row 5: *K5, K3tog, rep from * to end (17 [25] sts).
Next row 6: Work 1 row.

Small size only:
Next row 7: *K2, K2tog, rep from * to end (13 sts).

Next row 8: *P1, P2tog, rep from * to end (9 sts).

Large size only:
Next row 7: *K3, K3tog, rep from * to end (17 sts).
Next row 8: *P1, P2tog, rep from * to end (11 sts).
Next row 9: K3, K2tog, K3, K2tog, K1 (9 sts).
Next row 10: Work 1 row.

Both sizes:
Break the yarn, leaving a long tail. Thread the yarn through the remaining stitches. Pull up tight to create the crown and use the remaining yarn to sew up the hat.

Making up
Press as described on page 46.

Beaded make-up bag

This is the height of luxury in make-up bags. If you pull this out to find your lipstick, there's no doubt you'll look like a million dollars. Lined in velvet, it could also double up as a jewellery bag. It makes the perfect gift for someone special, particularly if you fill it with make-up, sweets, soaps or even jewels. The Cashmerino yarn makes it incredibly soft, but you can knit with any Aran-weight yarn.

EQUIPMENT

1 pair 5.5mm needles
362 beads
Lining
1 snap faster
1 knitted flower (see page 51 for instructions)

YARN

1 x 50g ball Debbie Bliss Cashmerino Aran, shade 603 Pink

TENSION

Using 5.5mm needles 18 sts x 24 rows = 10cm (4in) square.

ABBREVIATIONS

Pb (place bead) = bring yarn to front of work, bring bead up yarn to needle, push bead up tight to the needle, slip the next stitch purlwise, take yarn to back of work, knit 1.
Note: the method explaining beading on page 48 will place the bead in between the stitches. The method explained above is suitable for larger beads that sit on top of the stitch to give it a bobble effect.
K2tog (knit two stitches together)
P2tog (purl two stitches together)

METHOD

Knit in a combination of moss stitch and stocking stitch.

Cast on 34 sts.

Row 1: K1, P1 to end.

Row 2: P1, K1 to end. (These 2 rows form moss stitch.)

Row 3: K2, *Pb, K1*, rep from * to * until last 2 sts, K2.

Row 4: Purl. (These last 2 rows form stocking stitch.)

Row 5: K3, *Pb, K1*, rep from * to * until last st, K1.

Row 6: Purl.

Repeat last 6 rows until work measures 26.5cm (10¹/₂in).

Decreasing

1. K2tog. *K1, Pl*, rep from * to * until last 2 sts, K2tog (32sts).

2. K2tog. *K1, Pl*, rep from * to * until last 2 sts, K2tog (30sts).

3. K2tog. *Pb, K1*, rep from * to * until last 2 sts, K2tog (28sts).

4. P2tog. Purl to last 2 sts, P2tog (26sts).

5. K2tog. K1, *Pb, K1*, rep from * to * last 3 sts, K1, K2tog (24sts).

6. P2tog. Purl to last 2 sts, P2tog (22sts).

7. K2tog. *K1, Pl*, rep from * to * until last 2 sts, K2tog (20sts).

8. K2tog. *K1, Pl*, rep from * to * until last 2 sts, K2tog (18 sts).

9. K2tog, K2, *Pb, K1*, rep from * to * until last 2 sts, K2tog (16sts).

10. P2tog. Purl to last 2 sts, P2tog (14sts).

11. K2tog, K1, *Pb, K1*, rep from * to * until last 3 sts, K1, K2tog (12 sts).

12. P2tog. Purl to last 2 sts, P2tog (10sts).

13. K2tog. *K1, Pl*, rep from * to * until last 2 sts, K2tog (8 sts).

14. K2tog. *K1, Pl*, rep from * to * until last 2 sts, K2tog (6 sts).

15. Cast off.

Sew in ends.

Block and press.

Making up

1. Lay the knitted piece flat and measure a piece of lining 1cm (¹/₃in) bigger than the knitted piece to allow for the seam. Lay the front face of the lining to the front face of the knitted piece and machine-sew leaving, one side of one of the decreased edges open. When stitching, leave the edges of the knitted stitches free, so the sides can be sewn up later.

2. Turn the fabric inside out to reveal the right side of the knitted piece. At the open edge, tuck the lining under and hand-stitch the rest of the lining to the knitted piece.

3. Fold so that the right sides are facing and bring the bottom edge of the fabric up to 1cm (¹/₃in) below the point where decreasing starts and stitch the two side seams using the over-and-over method (see page 44).

4. Gently press the seams. Sew a snap fastener on the inside of the flap. Sew beads on to each side petal of the knitted flower and attach to the front of the bag flap.

Funky cushions

Both of these cushions have been knitted to show off the beautiful colours of this Colinette yarn. The Silkychic yarn used in Cushion 1 is so soft, silky and sumptuous, it feels as if you are knitting with feathers. The combination of Firecracker and Point Five yarn used in Cushion 2 simply sparkles with light and colour. The Firecracker yarn is just like satin to the touch and has an inviting fluffy texture.

CUSHION 1

EQUIPMENT
1 pair 5mm needles
1 x 40cm (16in) cushion pad
Four large buttons

YARN
2 x 100g hanks Colinette Silkychic, shade Gaugin

TENSION
Using 5mm needles 18 sts x 24 rows = 10cm (4in) square.

METHOD
Knit both panels in the same way, as follows:
Cast on 65 sts with 5mm needles and knit in garter stitch (knit every row) until work measures 40cm (16in).
Cast off.

Making up
1. Sew in ends.
2. Join knitted sections along 3 seams.
3. Turn inside out.
4. Put the cushion pad into the cover and stitch across the top to secure.
5. Attach buttons to decorate.

Make 4 pom-poms (see page 49), and attach them by sewing one pom-pom into each corner of the cushion.

  Patterns...Funky Fashions

Panel 2

CUSHION 2

EQUIPMENT

1 pair 10mm needles

1 pair 12mm needles

YARN

2 x 100g hanks Colinette Firecracker, shade Turquoise

1 x 100g hank Colinette Point Five, shade Paint Box

TENSION

Using 10mm needles with Firecracker yarn 8 sts x 12 rows = 10cm (4in) square.

Using 12mm needles with Point Five yarn 7 sts x 9 rows = 10cm (4in) square.

METHOD

Panel 1:

Cast on 40 sts with Firecracker yarn and 10mm needles and knit in stocking stitch throughout (knit one row, purl one row alternately).

Knit until work measures 40cm (16in).

Cast off.

Panel 2:

Cast on 35 sts with Point Five yarn and 12mm needles and knit in stocking stitch throughout (knit one row, purl one row alternately).

Knit until work measures 40cm (16in).

Cast off.

Making up

1. Sew in ends.
2. With right sides of the pieces facing, sew up 3 sides of the cushion.
3. Turn inside out.
4. Place the cushion pad inside the knitted pieces and stitch across the top to secure.
5. Thread a bodkin needle or a sewing needle with a large-enough eye to thread the Firecracker yarn.

Make 4 tassels (see page 50), and attach one to each corner of the cushion securely.

Button handbag

Once you've made this pretty button bag, others will be begging you to make more, so either pretend you bought it in a designer shop, or buy plenty of yarn and be prepared to knit for your friends and family for the next year. The most fun aspect about making this bag is rummaging in junk shops for the prettiest buttons. Any yarn can be used and it can be knitted to any size – just use the size needles that are recommended for the yarn.

EQUIPMENT
1 pair 4.5mm needles
Lining
1 snap fastener or Velcro fastening
80–100 buttons
Ribbon, 4cm (1¹/₂in) wide, 1.5m (60in) long

YARN
2 x 50g balls Rowan 4-ply Cotton, shade 129 Aegean (used in double thickness throughout)

TENSION
Using 4.5mm needles 18 sts x 25 rows = 10cm (4in) square.

METHOD
Cast on 45 sts.

Rows 1–40: Work in stocking stitch until work measures approx. 15.25cm (6in).
Rows 41–42: *K1, P1* repeat *to* to end of row. This sets moss stitch.
Rows 43–62: Continue in moss stitch for a further 20 rows until the moss stitch rows measure approx. 9cm (3¹/₂in).
Rows 63–104: Work in stocking stitch until total work measures approx. 38.5cm (15in).
Cast off.

Making up
Sew in ends.
Block and press.

Lining
1. Lay the knitted piece flat and measure a piece of lining fabric 1cm (¹/₃in) bigger than the knitted piece to allow for the seam. Lay the front face of the fabric to the front face of the knitted piece and machine-sew 3 sides, leaving the top seam open. When stitching, leave the edges of the knitted stitches free so the sides can be sewn up later.
2. Turn the fabric inside out to reveal the right side of the knitted piece. Fold in half with wrong side facing.
3. Stitch up the side seams of the bag, stitching the knitted pieces together.
4. Turn the top seam under by 2.5cm (1in) and stitch.
5. Turn each end of ribbon under by 2cm (³/₄in) and stitch 4 sides of the ribbon to inside the side seams at the top of the bag.

Finishing
1. Sew the buttons randomly on the front of the bag, sewing through the lining to secure the buttons in place.
2. Sew the snap fastener or Velcro fastening to the inside of the bag.
3. Tie the ribbon in a bow and sew the bow in place to secure the strap.

Dog jackets

Well, of course they get cold – especially the little cute ones with hardly any fur. One glance in a dog-walking zone tells you that dog jackets are now all the rage and no pooch should be seen without one. Purely for fashion's sake substitute a cotton yarn for this Merino one to make an alternative jacket – then your canine companion can look stylish in both the summer and winter months.

EQUIPMENT
1 pair 4mm needles
1 pair 4.5mm needles
1 set of 4 x 4.5mm double-pointed needles

YARN
Shark coat:
Yarn A: Debbie Bliss Merino DK, shade 104
2 x 50g balls (for small size), 2 x 50g balls (for medium size), 3 x 50g balls (for large size)
Yarn B: 1 x 50g ball Debbie Bliss Merino DK, shade 101

Pom-pom coat:
Debbie Bliss Merino DK, shade 301
2 x 50g balls (for small size), 2 x 50g balls (for medium size), 3 x 50g balls (for large size)
Colour oddments (for pom-poms)

TENSION
Using 4mm needles 22 sts x 28 rows = 10cm (4in) square.
Using 4.5mm needles 20 sts x 26 rows = 10cm (4in) square.

METHOD
The instructions are written for the small size. If changes are necessary for medium or larger sizes, the instructions are given in brackets.

For the shark coat

Neck ribbing:

Cast on 47 [61/85] sts with yarn A and 4mm needles.

Row 1: (Rs) K1 *P1, K1, rep from * to end.

Row 2: P1 *K1, Pl, rep from * to end.

Repeat these two rows K1, Pl, ribbing for a further 18 [20/22] rows ending on the 2nd row and increase 1 st in the middle of the last row, leaving you with 48 [62/86] sts. Break off yarn.

Change to 4.5mm needles and proceed in stocking stitch. You will need 2 separate balls of shade 101 (yarn B), so wind off half to split the ball in 2.

Row 1: Using yarn B, K3 [K6/K8], rejoin yarn A making sure you twist both colours to avoid a gap. Knit until the last 3 [6/8] sts. With the 2nd ball of yarn B, join yarn, twisting yarn A to avoid a gap, and K3 [K6/K8] sts in yarn B.

Row 2: Using yarn B, P3 [P6/P8]. Change to yarn A and purl until the last 3 [6/8] sts.

P3 [6/8] sts in yarn B.

Rows 3–7: Increase 1 st at each end of this and every following 4 rows, increasing your sts in yarn B and keeping 42 [50/78] sts between each end in yarn A, leaving you with 58 [72/104] sts.

Continue in stocking stitch, increasing 1 st at each end of following knit row and every alternate row until you have 68 [82/122] sts.

P1 row.

Leg openings:

Both leg sections are worked at the same time, using separate balls of yarn for each section.

Row 1: Rs facing, using yarn B, K7 [10/12], cast off 6 [6/10] sts.

In yarn A, K42 [50/78] (including stitch on needle after cast off).

In yarn B, cast off 6 [6/10] sts. Knit until the end of row.

Row 2: Beginning with a purl row, work 9 rows in stocking

stitch from cast off sts, ending with Rs facing for next row.

Joining row:

Knit 7 [10/12] sts, turn and cast on 6 [6/10] sts, turn, K42 [50/78] sts, turn, cast on 6 [6/10] sts, turn, knit to end of row, leaving you with 68 [82/122] sts.

Continue until work after neck ribbing measures 23cm [25.5/29cm] (9in [10/11½in]) ending with a purl row.

Place a marker at each end of last row.

Back shaping:

Rs facing, cast off 9 sts at beginning of next 2 rows, leaving you with 54 [64/96] sts.

Next row: K2tog, K until last 2 sts, K2tog.

Next row: Purl.

Repeat the last 2 rows until there are 36 [42/66] sts on needle (these will be yarn A).

Continue until work measures approx. 32cm [39/53cm] (12½in [15½/21in]) (or length required to base of tail) ending on a purl row.

Leave remaining 36 [42/66] sts on a stitch holder.

Sew neck seam to markers.

Back ribbing:

With rs facing and double-pointed needles using yarn A and yarn B yarn where necessary, pick up and knit on first needle 40 [56/72] sts along body from marker to back, on 2nd needle, K36 [42/66] sts from spare needle. On 3rd needle pick up and knit 40 [56/72] sts along opposite side of body to marker, making a total of 116 .

Place marker on 1st st. Work 8 rounds of K1, P1 ribbing.

Cast off loosely in rib.

Leg ribbing:

Stitches to be picked up around the leg opening.

With first double-pointed needle, pick up and knit 10 [12/14] sts around the leg opening. With 2nd double-pointed needle, pick up and knit 10 [12/14] sts, and with 3rd needle pick up and knit 10 [12/14] sts, leaving a total of 30 [36/42] sts.

Place marker on the first st. Work 10 rounds of K1, P1 ribbing.

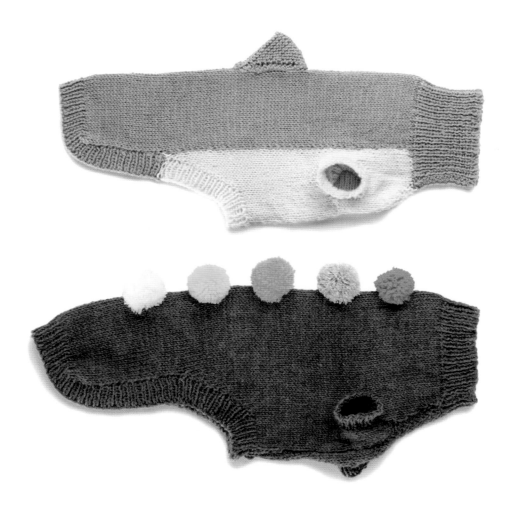

Cast off very loosely in rib. This is the ribbing for the dog's legs and will be too tight if you cast off tightly.

Repeat for 2nd leg opening.

To make fin:
Using 4.5mm needles and yarn A, cast on 3 sts.

Row 1: K1 yfwd K2 (4 sts).
Row 2 and every alternate row: Knit.
Row 3: K1 yfwd, K3 (5 sts).
Row 5: K1 yfwd, K4 (6 sts).
Row 7: K1 yfwd, K5 (7 sts).
Row 9: K1 yfwd, K6 (8 sts).
Row 11: K1 yfwd, K7 (9 sts).
Row 13: K1 yfwd, K8 (10 sts).
Row 15: K1 yfwd, K9 (11 sts).

Row 17: K1 yfwd, K10 (12 sts).
Row 19: K1 yfwd, K11 (13 sts).
Row 21: K1 yfwd, K12 (14 sts).
Row 22: Cast off 14 sts.

These 22 rows form the pattern.

For the pom–pom coat
Make as for the shark coat, but using one colour throughout.

Making up
Make 2 and sew them together.
Shark coat: Sew the fin on the appropriate place on the back of the dog coat.
Pom-pom coat: Make 5 small pom-poms (see page 49) and attach along the back of the coat.

Rose top

The fashionably close fit of this wide-ribbed vest is given a nostalgic, feminine touch by the delicate crochet trim. Be experimental and knit another version with the crochet in a contrast colour or texture such as a silky thread. The vest was originally intended to have a 'bootlace' ribbon threaded through it, but the roses caught my eye in a local haberdashery shop and seemed exactly right in form and colour. Why not make your own ribbon collection and rethread them to suit your mood?

EQUIPMENT
1 pair 3.25mm needles
Stitch holder
Row counter (optional)
Ribbon or braid, 1m (1yd) to thread as shown, 2m (2yd) if you want a bow at centre front.

YARN
Debbie Bliss Baby Cashmerino, shade 503 Pea Green

SIZES
Small sizes are given in the instructions with medium, large and Xlarge in brackets. This sizing is based on a gentle stretch to the knitting that opens the ribs out but is not a skin-tight fit. As the main fabric is so stretchy, this is only a rough guide to the finished size – the best method is to knit a large tension swatch and see what stretch you prefer before choosing the size to knit.

	SMALL UK 8–10	MEDIUM UK 12–14	LARGE UK 16–18	XLARGE UK 18–20
Bust:	81–86cm	91–97cm	102–108cm	110–115cm
	(32–34in)	(36–38in)	(40–42¹/₂in)	(43–45in)
Finished	86cm	94cm	104cm	112cm
bust:	(34in)	(37in)	(41in)	(45in)
Finished	46cm	48cm	50cm	52cm
length:	(18¹/₂in)	(19in)	(20in)	(21in)

YARN
(number of 50g/1oz balls)

SMALL UK 8–10	MEDIUM UK 12–14	LARGE UK 16–18	XLARGE UK 18–20
9	11	13	15

TENSION
Using 3.25mm needles with stocking stitch 25 sts x 34 rows = 10cm (4in) square.

METHOD
When you come to sew up this garment, you will need to turn both pieces back to front – so what was the right side when knitting becomes the inside. This makes knitting the holes easier, while also positioning lace holes at the centre front in a purl rib for a prettier threading of the ribbon.

Back
Cast on 108 [116/132/140] sts.

The main pattern, worked throughout:
Small and XL sizes:
*P4, K4, rep from * to last 4 sts, P4.
*K4, P4, rep from * to last 4 sts, K4. Rep these 2 rows.
M and L sizes:
*K4, P4, rep from * to last 4 sts, K4. Rep these 2 rows.
*P4, K4, rep from * to last 4 sts, P4.

Work 96 [97/97/86] rows in the main pattern until work measures 28.5cm [29/29.5/30cm] (11in [11¹/₂/12¹/₂in]) from cast on.

Underarm shaping:
Next row: Cast off 2 [2/3/8] sts at beginning of next 2 [2/2/2] rows.
Next row: Cast off 3 [3/2/1] sts at beginning of next 2 [2/2/2] rows.

  Patterns...Funky Fashions

Next row: Cast off 2 [2/3/1] sts at beginning of next 2 [2/2/2] rows.

Work 12 [14/12/12] rows, decreasing 1st at each end every 2 [2/2/2] rows.

Work 33 [37/47/49] rows straight.

Next row: Put in the lace holes across the middle 5 [5/5/5] knit stitch ribs. Working the lace holes on the knit stitch ribs is a simpler technique. Over the 4 sts on a 'right' side row this is worked as *yf, K2tog, K2tog into back of stitch, yrn*. Work 3 rows straight.

Next row: Make 2 lace holes in each of the first knit ribs that are outside the middle 5 [5/5/5] knit stitch ribs.

Shoulder and neck shaping:

Next row: Cast off 4 [4/5/4] sts on the outer edge at beginning of row and work 37 [36/40/43] sts main pattern. Place remaining sts on a stitch holder.

Next row: Turn work and cast off 8 [8/9/10] sts at the neck edge, K to end.

Next row: Cast off 4 [4/5/4] sts on the outer edge, knit to end.

Next row: Cast off 4 [4/5/3] sts at the neck edge and make 1 lace hole in the neck edge end of the next knit stitch rib out towards the edge, knit to end.

Next row: Cast off 4 [5/5/4] sts on the outer edge and knit to end.

Next row: Cast off 4 [5/5/4] sts at the neck edge and knit to end.

Next row: Work 4 rows casting off 4 [5/5/4] sts on the outer edge every other row.

Next row: Cast off remaining sts.

Opposite side shoulder and neck shaping:

Row 1: Return held stitches to needle and cast off the middle 9 [9/11/11] sts, knit main pattern to end.

Next row: Work 1 row.

Next row: Turn work and cast off 8 [8/9/10] sts at the neck edge, K to end of row.

Next row: Cast off 4 [4/5/4] sts on the outer edge, knit to end.

Next row: Cast off 4 [4/5/3] sts at the neck edge and make

1 lace hole in the neck edge end of the next knit stitch rib out towards the edge, knit to end.

Next row: Cast off 4 [5/5/4] sts on the outer edge and knit to end.

Next row: Cast off 4 [5/5/4] sts at the neck edge and knit to end.

Next row: Work 4 rows casting off 4 [5/5/4] sts on the outer edge every other row.

Next row: Cast off remaining sts.

Front

Work as back to row 117 [123/127/131] or until work measures 35cm [37/38/39cm] (14in [15/15/15½in]) from cast-on edge.

Next row: Make lace holes across the middle 5 [5/5/5] knit ribs.

Next row: Work 3 rows.

Next row: Work 1 row, making 1 lace hole (yf, K2tog) at the central side of one knit stitch rib preceding and following the centre 5.
Next row: Work 1 row.

Neck shaping:
Next row: Knit 33 [36/40/42] sts and place remaining stitches on a stitch holder.
Next row: Cast off 2 [2/2/3] sts at beginning (neck end) of row, K to end.
Next row: Work 1 row, making a lace hole (K2tog into back, yrn) in the outer end of the same knit stitch rib out from the centre 5 (this 'pairs' the hole made 4 rows earlier).
Next row: Work 5 [5/5/5] rows, casting off 2 [2/2/2] sts at beginning (neck end) of the first and every 2 [2/2/2] rows.
Next row: Work 1 row, making 1 lace hole (yf, K2tog) in the end nearest the neck of the next knit stitch rib out from the last one.
Next row: Work 2 [2/2/2] rows, casting off 1 [2/2/2] sts every 2 [2/2/2] rows.
Next row: Work 4 [4/4/4] rows, decreasing 1 [1/1/1] st every 2 [2/4/1] rows.
Next row: Work 1 row, making a lace hole (K2tog into back, yrn) in the outer end of the same knit stitch rib out from the last one (this 'pairs' the hole made 4 rows earlier).
Next row: Work 5 [5/5/5] rows, decreasing 1 [1/1/1] st at the neck edge every 3 [2/4/2] rows.
Next row: Work 1 row, making a lace hole (K2tog into back, yrn) directly above the last hole.
Next row: Work 2 [2/2/2] rows, decreasing 1st every 2 [2/2/2] rows.
Next row: Work 5 rows straight.
Next row: Work 1 row, making a lace hole (K2tog into back, yrn) directly above the last hole.
Next row: Work 2 [6/8/10] rows straight.

Shoulder shaping:
Next row: Cast off 4 [4/5/4] sts at shoulder edge, K to end.
Next row: Work 4 [4/4/4] rows casting off 4 [5/5/4] sts at shoulder edge every other row.
Next row: Cast off 4 sts at shoulder edge, making a lace hole

(K2tog into back, yrn) directly above the last hole.
Next row: Work 4 [4/4/4] rows, casting off 4 [4/5/5] sts at shoulder edge every other row.
Next row: Work 1 row.
Next row: Cast off remaining sts.

Opposite neck and shoulder shaping:
Row 1: Return remaining sts back on to needle, cast off the centre 16 sts and knit to end.
Next row: Work 1 row.
Next row: Cast off 2 [2/2/3] sts at beginning (neck end) of row, K to end.
Next row: Work 1 row, making a lace hole (K2tog into back, yrn) in the outer end of the same knit stitch rib out from the centre 5 (this 'pairs' the hole made 4 rows earlier).
Next row: Work 5 [5/5/5] rows, casting off 2 [2/2/2] sts at beginning (neck end) of 1st and every 2 [2/2/2] rows.
Next row: Work 1 row, making 1 lace hole (yf, K2tog) in the end nearest the neck of the next knit stitch rib out from the last one.
Next row: Work 2 [2/2/2] rows, casting off 1 [2/2/2] st every 2 [2/2/2] rows.
Next row: Work 4 [4/4/4] rows, decreasing 1 [1/1/1] st every 2 [2/4/1] rows.
Next row: Work 1 row, making a lace hole (K2tog into back, yrn) in the outer end of the same knit stitch rib out from the last one (this 'pairs' the hole made 4 rows earlier).
Next row: Work 5 [5/5/5] rows, decreasing 1 [1/1/1] st at the neck edge every 3 [2/4/2] rows.
Next row: Work 1 row, making a lace hole (K2tog into back, yrn) directly above the last hole.
Next row: Work 2 [2/2/2] rows, decreasing 1st every 2 [2/2/2] rows.
Next row: Work 5 rows straight.
Next row: Work 1 row, making a lace hole (K2tog into back, yrn) directly above the last hole.
Next row: Work 2 [6/8/10] rows straight.

Shoulder shaping:
Next row: Cast off 4 [4/5/4] sts at shoulder edge, K to end.
Next row: Work 4 [4/4/4] rows casting off 4 [5/5/4] sts at shoulder edge every other row.

Next row: Cast off 4 sts at shoulder edge, making a lace hole (K2tog into back, yrn) directly above the last hole.

Next row: Work 4 [4/4/4] rows, casting off 4 [4/5/5] sts at shoulder edge every other row.

Next row: Work 1 row.

Next row: Cast off remaining sts.

Sleeves

These are the same for all sizes.

Sew shoulder seams with mattress stitch, matching ribs carefully. Note: Do not steam this garment if it is knitted in the specified yarn as the rib looses its elasticity when steamed.

Count up from the underarm on the armhole edge, and put a marker 10 rows up from the end of the shaping on both front and back. To make the pick-up even, mark your armhole again halfway between this marker and the shoulder seam. This gives you 4 equal sections to divide your stitches between.

Evenly pick up 44 [52/52/60] sts along the complete edge from front to back. (Numbers may vary with your personal knitting tension, but as a rough guide based on my tension, picking up 5 sts across 7 rows will give this result.)

Knit the main pattern across these sts, casting off 4 sts on alternate rows until there are 3 ribs left on the needles, Knit 1 row, then cast these off.

Making up

1. Sew the completed garment pieces together underarm with mattress stitch.

2. Crochet a basic crochet stitch completely around the sleeve edges and neck edge. Do not stretch the edge, but neither should you pull it tight.

3. Next, crochet a 6-chain loop along the edge of the base crochet, catching the chain into the edge every 3rd crochet stitch so the loops are forced out into a scallop effect.

4. Sew in the ends and thread a ribbon of your choice through the lace holes.

Yarn tote bag

This bag has been made using a cheap woollen blanket from a charity shop that has been dyed bright pink with a washing-machine dye. It gives a really convincing impression of a hand-felted bag. Make sure you buy a blanket that is 100 per cent natural fibre as the dye doesn't work on synthetic fibres. The hotter you wash it, the more felted it looks. If you make it up with smaller dimensions, it also makes a really hip handbag.

EQUIPMENT

1 blanket
1 pack of Dylon machine-dye (shown in Deep Pink)
Lining fabric
Sewing thread
Sewing-machine or hand-sewing needle
Pins
T-shirt transfer
30.5cm (12in) piece of light cotton, slightly larger than the image
Computer, scanner and colour printer
Iron

METHOD

1. Cut a piece of fabric 40.5 x 79cm (16 x 31in) for the bag and 2 pieces of fabric 11.5 x 63.5cm (4$\frac{1}{2}$ x 25in) for the straps.
2. Cut a piece of lining the same size as the main piece of fabric.
3. Stitch the wrong side of the lining to the wrong side of the main fabric, so you have one piece of fabric.
4. Fold the fabric in half inside out, so the fold forms the bottom of the bag and it measures 40.5 x 39.5cm (16 x 15$\frac{1}{2}$in).
5. Stitch up the sides using, leaving a 1.5cm ($\frac{5}{8}$in) seam (1).

6. While the bag is still inside out, turn the top edge over 0.5cm ($\frac{1}{4}$in) and press. Fold again another 2.5cm (1in) and stitch 1.5cm ($\frac{5}{8}$in) from the fold (2). If you are using a blanket or a thick fabric, you may need to hand-stitch these seams.
7. To make the bag square at the bottom, keep the bag inside out, fold the side seam against the bottom seam and stitch a 10cm (4in) line at the bottom of the triangle (3). The bag should now look like it has two little ears.
8. To make the handles, fold the 2 smaller pieces of fabric lengthwise right side facing. Sew a seam along the longest edge and one of the short ends, leaving one of the seams open. Turn the right side out (it is useful to use a knitting needle to poke the fabric through gently). Stitch the other seam (4).
9. Attach the handles 6cm (2$\frac{1}{2}$in) in from each side seam. Stitch a rectangle to secure the handles (5).
10. Turn the bag right side out.

Image transfer

1. Find an image from your computer with which to decorate the bag.
2. Download and print on to a T-shirt transfer. Make sure you print with a mirror image for any text you want to print.
3. Iron the image on to a light piece of cotton, cut and stitch to neaten the edges and stitch in place on to the front of the bag using a zig-zag or decorative stitch.
4. Leave the top end open and use as a pocket for scissors, tape, stitch holders, sewing-up needle or mobile phone.

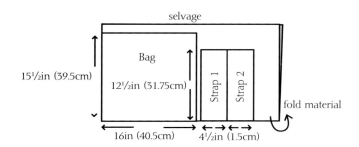

selvage

Bag

15½in (39.5cm)

12½in (31.75cm)

Strap 1

Strap 2

fold material

16in (40.5cm)

4½in (1.5cm)

1.
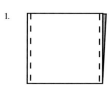

2

¼in (0.5cm)

1in (2.5cm)

⅝in (1.5cm)

3.
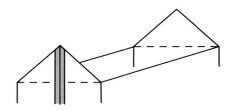

4.

5.
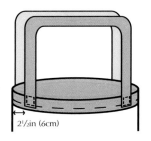

2½in (6cm)

Needle udder

It is so easy to lose your needles, so why not try making this simple needle case to carry around your most commonly used needles so you can always find the size you need?

EQUIPMENT
Cow fur fabric
Pink lining fabric
Tailor's chalk
Pink and black thread and sewing needles
Snap fastener
5 daisy buttons
0.5m (20in) cotton-covered elastic rope

METHOD
1. Cut a piece of lining 51 x 127cm (20 x 50in) (1).
2. Measure 71cm (28in) from one of the short edges, making a line with tailor's chalk. Fold the fabric from one short edge to this line, making a 35.5cm (14in) fold (2).
3. With tailor's chalk mark a line 20.4cm (8in) from the fold across the fabric. Starting at the 20.4cm (8in) line, mark a semi-circle towards the centre of the fold (3).
4. Sew the arch of the semi-circle (4).
5. Trim the excess off corners (5).
6. Turn right side out and press.
7. At the opposite short edge, sew a 2.5cm (1in) hem (6).
8. From the bottom of the 2.5cm (1in) hem, fold the fabric 30.5cm (12in) (7).
9. Sew the side (long) edges from the bottom end to the beginning of the semi-circle (flap) (8).
10. Sew straight lines of varying widths to form about 10 needle pockets (9).
11. Cut a piece of fur fabric 38cm x 56cm (15 x 22in). Lay the lining on the wrong side of the fur. Turn the fur 2.5cm (1in) over the 3 straight sides of the lining to form a neat edge (10). Sew in place (11).
12. Turn the fabric over. Secure the flap to the fur by sewing a straight line along the final raw edge, taking care not to stitch the needle pockets closed (12).
13. Secure the fastner to the flap and to the corresponding opposite on the needle pockets. Sew a button on top of the flap to decorate and hide the snap fastener thread.
15. Cut the elastic rope into 2 equal pieces.
16. Thread 2 daisy buttons on to one of the elastic pieces and sew the ends of elastic together.
17. Sew one of these buttons to one edge of the roll, wrap the elastic round the roll and secure by looping the second button over the first.
18. Repeat with the other 2 buttons and elastic for the other side.

Patterns...Funky Fashions

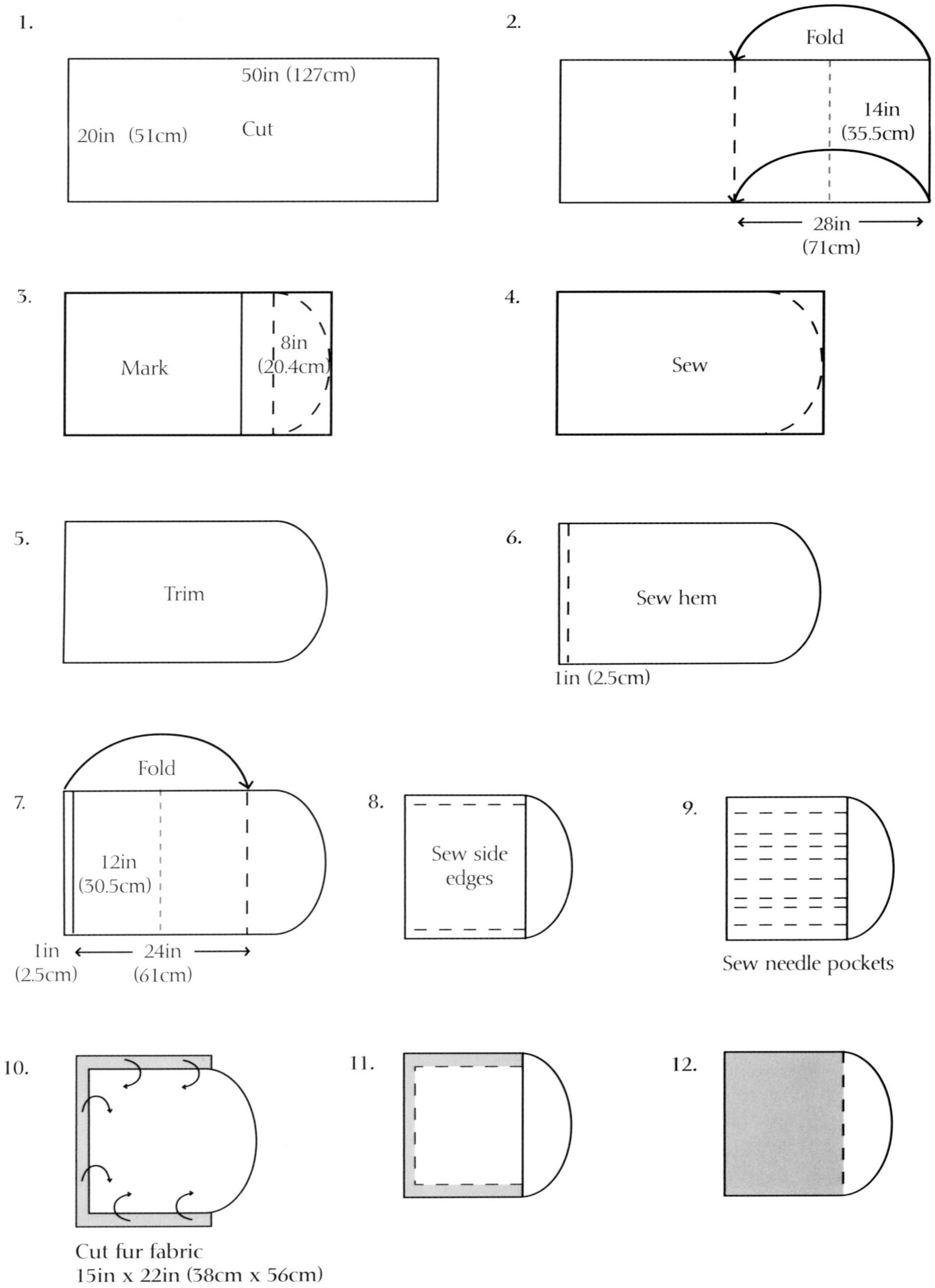

1.

50in (127cm)

20in (51cm)   Cut

2.

Fold

14in
(35.5cm)

28in
(71cm)

3.

Mark   8in
(20.4cm)

4.

Sew

5.

Trim

6.

Sew hem

1in (2.5cm)

7.

Fold

12in
(30.5cm)

1in   24in
(2.5cm)   (61cm)

8.

Sew side
edges

9.

Sew needle pockets

10.

Cut fur fabric
15in x 22in (38cm x 56cm)

11.

12.

20 mistakes that every knitter should make

1   Knit one sleeve longer than the other.

2. You must drop a stitch so that it runs the whole way down your garment, which inevitably starts to unravel.

3. Knit the neck so tight that you can't get it over your head.

4. Knit the neck so loose that it shows your cleavage.

5. Knit something so itchy that it is never worn or means your boyfriend won't give you a hug because you're too itchy – a real passion killer.

6. Knit something fabulous and never sew it up, Throw it in the loft and don't see it for 20 years, by which time it'll be moth-eaten and home to refugee rats with a family of 56 aunts and uncles.

7. Don't count your stitches, so that instead of having straight lines your scarf looks like hour-glasses stitched together.

8. Offer to knit a new boyfriend a woolly jumper – then he'll be scared off and will run a mile, because of too much commitment on your part.

9. Try to adapt something your knitting experience isn't ready for. Always follow the instructions, they are there to help.

10. Sew the wrong side to the right side. So you have the inside sleeve attached to the outside back.

11. Start knitting something for somebody's baby, take 18 years and give it to them just as they are about to leave home for university.

12. Wash your garment and then promptly shrink it after spending 10 years making it.

13. Knit a jumper for a relative as a gift without measuring them – Uncle Charlie always wanted a knitted dress.

14. Knit your partner a reindeer or snowman jumper for Christmas.

15. Let your cat sleep on your lap while knitting, then when it gets up find cat dribble all over your cashmere masterpiece.

16. Knit Fairisle and get the pattern totally muddled up so your garment looks like a sea of mangled colour or Joseph's technicolour raincoat.

17. Go to Knit Nights every Monday and undo your knitting more than you actually knit.

18. Knit your stitches so tight that you can't get them off the needle.

19. Knit a bikini and swim in it. (Knitting swimming trunks is definitely not a mistake – it'll give you a laugh.)

20. Show your mother your knitting. She'll be of the old school of 1970s and 1980s feminists and will think you've let the side down.

Stockists

UK

Beads Unlimited
PO Box 1
Hove
Sussex BN3 3SG
www.beadsunlimited.co.uk
email: mailbox@beadsunlimited.co.uk
Tel: 01273 740777

Debbie Bliss
www.debbieblissonline.com
email: jane@designeryarns.uk.com

Colinette Yarns Ltd
Banwy Workshops
Llanfair Caereinion
Powys, Wales SY21 0SG
www.colinette.com
email: info@colinette.com
Tel: 01938 810128

Designer Yarns Ltd
Units 8-10 Newbridge Industrial Estate
Pitt Street
Keighley
West Yorkshire BD21 4PQ
www.designeryarns.uk.com

email: jane@designeryarns.uk.com
Tel: 01535 664222

Injabulo Buttons
(hand-made ceramic buttons)
Broom Cottage
Ashton
Oundle
Peterborough PE8 5LD
01832 274881
www.injabulo.com
Email: info@injabulo.com

John Lewis
For a list of stores visit:
www.johnlewis.com

Laughing Hens
PO Box 176
St Leonards on Sea
East Sussex TN38 0GZ
www.laughinghens.com
email: info@laughinghens.com
Tel: 01424 202010

Rowan Yarns
Green Lane Mill
Holmfirth
West Yorkshire HD9 2DX

www.knitrowan.co.uk
email: info@knitrowan.co.uk
Tel: 01484 681881

USA

Knitting Fever Inc
35 Debevoise Avenue
Roosevelt, NY 11575
www.knittingfever.com

The Knitting Garden
25 Longmeadow Road
Uxbridge, MA 01569
www.theknittinggarden.com
email: Elizabeth@theknittinggarden.com
Tel: 888 381 9276

Purl
137 Sullivan Street
New York, NY 10012
Tel: 212 420 8796
www.store.purlsoho.com
email: customerservice@purlsoho.com

Useful addresses and other interesting knitting places

The Crafts Council
44a Pentonville Road
Islington
London
N1 9BY
020 7278 7700
www.craftscouncil.org.uk

Knit Café
8441 Melrose Avenue
Los Angeles, CA 90069
Tel: 323 658 5648
www.knitcafe.com
email: knitcafe@aol.com

Knitting & Crochet Guild (UK)
PO Box HH1
Leeds
LS8 2YB
www.knitting-and-crochet-guild.org.uk

The Knitting Guild of America (US)
PO Box 3388
Zanesville, OH 43702-3388
www.tkga.com
email Tkga@tkga.com

Vogue Knitting
www.vogueknitting.com

Cast Off
London
www.castoff.info
email: info@castoff.info

Extreme Knitters
www.xtremeknitting.com

Knitty Magazine
http://www.knitty.com/
ISSUEwinter04/index.html

Knitting software resources:
http://knitting.about.com/
library/weekly/aa071397.htm

Try this knitting quiz to test your knowledge:

http://www.funtrivia.com/
playquiz.cfm?qid=6151&origin

PART ONE

New-Age Crochet

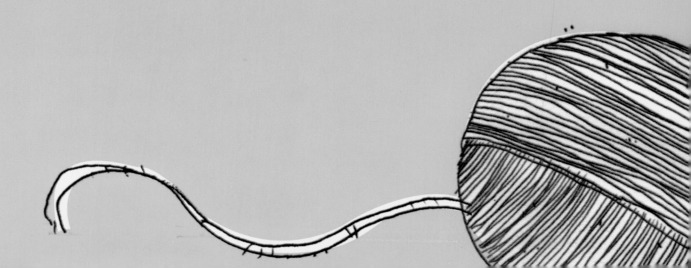

Crochet's back in the limelight

Crochet is losing its old-fashioned reputation. You may associate the craft with black-clad grannies of southern Europe sitting in their doorways in the evening sunshine, adeptly crocheting doilies on which to put their candlesticks. Yet now, with the increasing demand for hand-crafted accessories and domestic items, crochet is re-inventing itself for the 21st century.

Crochet on the Rowan stand at the Knitting and Stiching Show, London.

Reinventing crochet

In the year 2000 Rowan Yarns, realising that there was a younger market who were coming back to crafts, brought out an exciting new range of thick superchunky yarn called Big Wool and Biggy Print. Their range of stylish mini-books, full of stunning fashion photography, helped stimulate knitting and crochet as popular crafts. Yarns from breeds of sheep such as the merino with an ultra-soft fleece are being mixed with real luxury fibres from breeds such as alpaca, cashmere and angora to create new and versatile yarns. So shades of yarn are no longer defined by shiny acrylics in primary colours.

In the USA crochet is more popular than knitting, 80–90 per cent of people who crochet make throws (afghans); they are usually made from squares that are joined together, so it feels as if you have achieved something in a short space of time and they are easy to work. Most people who crochet also tend to knit, the two crafts go hand in hand.

In the UK knitting still dominates over crochet, although British yarn companies are now incorporating crochet patterns into their knitting pattern books. British yarn company Rowan have recently added 'crochet' to the titles of their popular magazines and the titles now read: 'Knitting and Crochet patterns' instead of just 'Knitting patterns'.

Designs for garments tend to be knitted or a combination of both knitting and crochet. Knitting is generally a tighter fabric and crochet a little more open and best suited to fashion and home accessories such as scarves, hats, throws, bags, cushion covers and is also often used as an attractive edging for a knitted piece.

People are turning back to home crafts as an antidote to a harsh computerised world. Career women are now reclaiming their domestic heritage. By day they strike lucrative deals: they are well-educated, smart and everything the feminists of the 1960s dreamed of. By night, after a long day at the office, the career woman throws on her apron, bakes home-made muffins and trots along to her local knitting and crochet club.

In spite of the march of Ikea-style minimalism, chintz and gingham never go out of fashion, forming part of a security blanket that we all need. Whatever their lifestyle choice, women won't abandon their natural nesting instincts. In the USA Tupperware-style parties are making a comeback and knitting and crochet clubs are having the same impact. Housewives, working mums, single women and career women are getting together to rediscover this ancient bond. They meet in each other's homes, in cafés, in fashionable bars and pubs to wind down and relax with a glass of wine or

Rowan Slingbag

a hot chocolate. These women may well be able to afford luxury knitting items, but prefer the pleasure of knitting or crocheting their own.

In the USA Stitch 'n' Bitch groups have been set up throughout the country. The craze was started by Debbie Stoller, the well-known author and journalist, who sees knitting and crochet as a representation of a new age of feminism. Mostly, though, women join the groups for the social scene rather than for any strong political motivation. They meet, chat, and swap patterns and yarn. It seems that with family groups being more scattered, women turn to hobby groups to form their own community networks.

The increasing popularity of humble, home-making activities such as knitting and crochet is linked to the fact that we live in more uncertain times. People are turning to their homes, places where they feel safe, and where the smell of freshly baked bread, floral interiors and the sound of clicking needles gives comfort from the disturbing images filtered into our homes by the media.

Who crochets?

Anybody interested in creative, individual work will be interested in crochet. On the back of the home DIY revolution, people are making quick and easy projects that fit with modern-day items. There is a huge trend in wearing anything that is home-made. Bored of high-street fashions, people are looking for items that make them stand out in a crowd and at a fraction of the price of couture-house and catwalk styles. In the high street, too, you'll find crochet everywhere, particularly crocheted accessories, such as hats, bags, scarves and the ever-present poncho. There are even crocheted thongs and shoes.

Men who crochet

In the USA men crochet and nobody bats an eyelid. It has become perfectly acceptable to sit next to a man in the subway, or in a bar, who is crocheting something for his wife. It even seems to be a good way of attracting women if you're single – a woman always likes a sensitive type and crochet is a very tactile craft. You are, however, less likely to find a man crocheting in the UK, where crochet is still a mainly female pastime. In the USA, there is an online yahoo group, Men Who Crochet, which has its own podcast crochet show that broadcasts every week with news, tips and general crochet chat. This can be either listened to on the Internet or downloaded onto your MP3 player. It seems that crochet has a mathematical element to it which suits the male brain, and the rhythmic craft has attracted even the butchest men, such as Ian Johnson from Boise State Broncos football team in Idaho, who crochets and sells team hats for his fellow players and fans. His nickname is 'Crochet boy'. 'How can you tease a guy if he's making stuff for you?', one of his team-mates said.

Crochet in fashion

Crochet is now scattered all over the catwalks and every one of the big fashion houses seems to have crochet in some form in their collection. Just flick through *Vogue* and *Elle* and you'll find pages with crochet everywhere. There is an exhibition in Italy called *Pitti Filati*, that takes place every season, to show current and future trends in knitwear, which has been packed out with buyers from Prada, Louis Vuitton and Stella McCartney, who are all using hand knitting and crochet in their collections.

Celebrity crocheters

Even celebrities are taking up knitting and crochet. The combination of having extended gaps between shoots or recording sessions and crochet being such a portable craft makes it seem an ideal way to pass the time. Celebrities such as Julia Roberts, Gerri Halliwell, Daryl Hannah, Goldie Hawn and Sarah Jessica Parker have all been spotted proudly with hook and yarn between their fingers.

It is a well-known fact that E.M. Forster, when hanging out with the Bloomsbury Set in the 1930s, became totally hooked on crochet. So you are in good company.

Seung Hee Lee

What is crochet?

Simple crochet

Crochet is a series of knots intertwined with a hook that make a piece of knotted textile. A succession of loops are pulled through each other to make an intricate, yet beautiful piece of fabric.

Any lengths of textile can be used to crochet. Traditionally cotton was used for intricate lace work, but now thicker, chunkier yarns are more commonly used to create fashionable bags, accessories and garments. String, rag or leather can also be used. You will often find a beautiful bag or summer hat crocheted in the kind of twine that can easily be bought from your local hardware shop.

Crochet is so much easier than knitting. There are only three basic stitches, with others just variations of those three. Often children are taught crochet before knitting – it's a lot less daunting to just have one short hook and it's easier to navigate than using needles. Best of all, if you make a mistake with crochet you can just take out the hook and pull the work back to the previous stitch and only have one stitch to pick up again, instead of a whole mound of stitches on a knitting needle.

Crochet projects are easy to carry around, so you can crochet anywhere – on trains, planes, buses and car journeys (though not when you're driving!). It is a very rhythmic action and can be quite mesmerising to watch. Most crochet projects are quite small. Large garments tend to be knitted rather than crocheted and the other big items such as throws (afghans) tend to be made up of small crocheted squares joined together.

Filet Crochet

This type of crochet is popular with those who want to create a design on an item. This is a technique based on a simple network with a regular, square grid made up of treble and chain stitches. Patterns are shown in the form of a squared chart. The patterns can have very intricate designs: flowers, geometric patterns, lettering and sometimes even whole scenes.

Tunisian crochet

This is a particular type of crochet that is worked back and forth without turning the work. Tunisian crochet is worked with a longer hook than the normal crochet hook, it's required to hold loops that are made on the first half of the row before working them off on the second half of the row. Tunisian crochet makes a very dense fabric.

Crochet in art

Textile arts are now becoming tremendously popular. There was recently a show that ran in London at the Crafts Council gallery called Knit 2 Together, featuring some stunning textiles using both knitting and crochet as a medium for art.

Crochet is ideally suited as an art form; it produces big loops and can easily create a sense of texture and design.

Git-Ying Tse

There are specific crochet artists who are exhibiting their work throughout the world. It seems the popularity of textiles is continuing to expand with the university and college intake of textile graduates showing a dramatic rise in recent years.

Freeform crochet

This is a unique way of self expression in the craft, where the crocheted fabric takes on a life of its own. The technique of freeform crochet is used to create a piece of crocheted artwork. Structures are in two and three dimensions and the piece is made using different yarns and textiles to create a beautiful individual piece of art.

Detail from green jumper, Seung Hee Lee

1950s

Crochet through the decades

Crochet quiz

Now you've read a little bit about the subject, try our crochet quiz for fun. Don't let the clues put you off; the answers are in your crochet knowledge and are commonly used crochet terms.

1. What traditional crochet items stop your vases from scratching your polished tables?

2. What looks like a musical note but has more to do with hooks and loops?

3. Which sheep has an extremely soft fleece and likes to dance the flamenco?

4. What does Peter Pan's arch-enemy use for one-handed crochet?

5. Which useful instruction shows the way to sail or a patient's progress?

6. Who knows which Peruvian animal this is?

7. What do shy actors use for nude scenes or dangerous stunts?

8. What do you have to do to get your boat gently down the stream?

9. Which ripping old-style tale may be named because the teller can spin it out?

10. What sharp pain do you get if you run too fast after sitting and crocheting for a long while?

11. Boys with high voices. Maybe three of them?

12. What isn't round and has four equal sides?

13. Matisse was fond of them and they are an essential instruction.

14. What do you and your friends do with your hands when singing a New Year's song?

15. What major brand of yarns and patterns produces the popular superchunky yarns: Biggy Print and Big Wool?

16. Contrary to the flat earth theory, what shape is the planet Earth?

17. What's a bright and colourful cheerleader accessory?

18. What Dracula's title?

19. What sounds like an urgent activity using dried flowers between two sheets of paper?

20. What kind of gang is famous for its convictions?

Answers

1. Doilies
2. Crochet
3. Merino
4. Hook
5. Chart
6. Alpaca
7. Double
8. Row
9. Yarn
10. Stitch
11. Treble
12. Square
13. Patterns
14. Join
15. Rowan Yarns
16. Round
17. Pom pom
18. Count
19. Pressing
20. Chain

PART TWO

What you need...

... and what to do with it

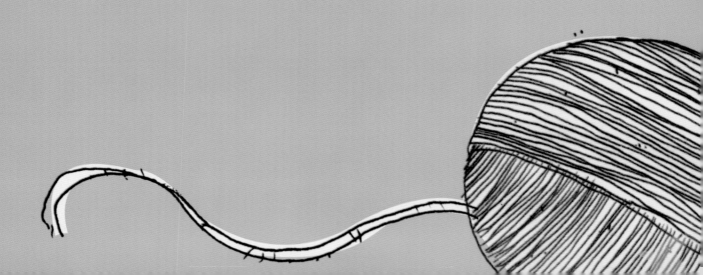

> You can crochet with almost anything that takes the form of a long, continuous line, is reasonably flexible and can be put around a crochet hook. There is a heap of new yarns available with which to experiment. You can even use string, wire, leather or strips of fabric.

YARN TYPES

The many varieties of sumptuous yarn that are now available make crochet a delightful pastime. Luxury yarns such as alpaca, angora, cashmere and mohair are being mixed with the soft fleece of the merino sheep (originally from Spain but now raised all over Europe, Australia and the US). In the past woollen fabrics were often rough and itchy, but the new popularity of luxury yarns means that people are willing to pay more for their soft, sumptuous feel. Colour palettes have also changed from the bright, luminescent colours that were typical of acrylic yarns to match the natural and subtle colours that people are now choosing for their home décor.

Wool

There are many types of wool sourced from different breeds of sheep and there are, in turn, many types of fleece with varying levels of softness. Having become accustomed to the comfort that was introduced by the use of manmade fibres, consumers are now demanding softer, natural wool in an abundance of different thicknesses, from fine 4 plys to superchunky thick yarns that come in a variety of plain and fancy textures.

Sheep breeds with fleeces that create fine wools include Delaine Merino, Shetland and Debouillet. In the UK the fleece of the Blue Leicester sheep is often mixed with other

less fine fleeces to provide the required softness. Medium wools include Dorset, Suffolk, Shropshire and Navajo Churro; long wools include Lincoln, Cotswold, Teeswater and Shetland. Coarse wools tend to be used for other functions such as carpets or wool insulation.

If you buy a woollen garment that has been hand knitted or crocheted in South America, it is sometimes rough on the skin and may even have bits of wood and straw tangled up in it that haven't been removed at the fleece combing stage; it seems the South Americans are less concerned with the roughness of some garments, maybe because they use these as jackets or over-garments and wear something else underneath them. However, the alpaca is native to South America and has an incredibly soft and luscious fleece and is becoming more popular throughout Europe and the US as a hand knitting yarn.

Silk

One of the more expensive yarns with which to crochet, silk yarn is often mixed with wool, creating a distinctive sheen and a soft and silky feel. Silk creates a light and luxurious yarn that makes lovely summer wraps and tops. It feels very rich to the touch and is often worth the extra expense.

Cotton

Cotton is traditionally used for finer items such as doilies or lacy tablecloths. Double-knit cotton is a thicker cotton that is easy to crochet and can be useful for cushions or throws and gives a thicker more plump feel than fine cotton. If you want a softer quality use wools or silky yarns.

Ribbon yarn

This yarn comes in all thicknesses and makes a very soft fabric. Light and cool, it is ideal for summer tops, cushions and throws.

Eyelash yarn/hairy yarns

Although they have become popular in recent years, eyelash yarns are not ideally suited to crochet. This type of yarn tends to hide the stitch so it is difficult to see the stitch structure in the fabric. The hairs in the yarn also lock into each other making

Fancy yarns

Any type of yarn that has been spun differently to form a curly or avant-garde look is called a fancy yarn. Some of these are spun with a mixture of fabric and wool to give an unusual effect.

String

A strong, firm material, string can look at home in any modern interior, particularly when used to crochet containers, runners and mats.

Rags

Use torn-up fabric to make rugs, bags, mats or garments.

Leather strips

With a glossy sheen, leather is very durable and can be effectively used for stylish interior accessories such as floor cushions or containers.

Raffia

A fun fabric for crocheting, raffia is the perfect material for making table mats and coasters. It comes in many colours as well as natural shades.

YARN THICKNESSES

Yarn is available in the following thicknesses. When practising new crochet techniques, it is easier to avoid using fine yarns

such as lurex and 4 ply, the double knits and aran are ideal because they're easier to handle.

4 ply

An ideal yarn for light garments and one that is often used for baby clothes and summer tops.

Double knitting (dk)

Providing a good general thickness of yarn, double knitting yarn is easy to crochet with. It takes a small to medium-sized hook that is easy to handle and is useful for all kinds of projects.

Aran

Another yarn with a general application, aran is thicker than double knitting and tends to be used for projects that require more warmth. Easy to handle, it is a good yarn for a beginner.

Chunky

Providing a warm, winter thickness of wool, a chunky yarn crochets quickly and is ideal for hats, scarves and gloves.

Superchunky

The popularity of this thick yarn is largely responsible for the recent revival in knitting and crochet. A superchunky garment is generally crocheted with a super-thick-size hook. Perfect for those who want to crochet a hat or scarf in one evening.

★ How to read a label

Yarn labels contain all sorts of useful information. Although it's tempting to fling the label away in your haste to get going on your crochet, you should definitely hold on to it for a while. You may, for example, run out of yarn and need an extra ball, in which case the label will tell you the exact dye-lot number and shade number you need – then you can get back to your supplier for an identical match.

The label gives washing and pressing instructions, vital for keeping your crochet in good condition. It also gives you the recommended tension and needle sizes to suit the thickness of the yarn.

The basic information on the label will have the brand name, the type of yarn, such as dk (double knitting) or aran, and the name of the range, such as Cashmerino Aran or Soft Tweed.

★ Crochet equipment

Crochet is probably one of the most unencumbered crafts in terms of equipment. A small hook, a pair of sharp scissors, some yarn and you'll be off to a good start.

HOOKS

Crochet hooks come in all sizes. Wool hooks start at around 2.00mm and go up to the superchunky size 15.00mm. The smaller sizes tend to be metal and as they get bigger they change to plastic. Wooden and bamboo hooks are available in the middle sizes and these have become popular in recent years. When buying bamboo hooks, it is wise to invest in quality brands to ensure the hook has a highly smooth finish. Most hooks will have a flat finger hold in the middle to help you achieve an even tension.

Very tiny steel hooks are used for fine cotton threads – these can be size 0.60mm or less. A Tunisian hook is longer than a standard crochet hook and looks like a cross between a knitting needle and a crochet hook.

Different countries use different sizing units for hooks. The conversion chart on the right shows how the sizes convert from metric sizes to US sizes, as well as the old UK sizes.

HOOK SIZE CONVERSION CHART

Metric	US	old UK
0.60mm	14 steel	–
0.75mm	12 steel	–
1.00mm	11 steel	–
1.50mm	8 steel	–
1.75mm	6 steel	–
2.00mm	B/1	14
2.50mm	C/2	12
3.00mm	D/3	10
3.50mm	E/4	9
4.00mm	F/5	8
4.50mm	G/6	7
5.00mm	H/8	6
5.50mm	I/9	5
6.00mm	J/10	4
6.50mm	–	3
7.00mm	K/10.5	2
8.00mm	L/11	–
9.00mm	M/13	–
10.00mm	N/15	–
12.00mm	O/P13	–
15.00mm	Q	–
20.00mm	S	–

What you need… and what to do with it

PINS

Straight pins with coloured ends should be used for blocking and checking tension. Avoid ordinary pins with steel ends, which will get lost in the yarn. Safety pins are very useful for crochet; a small version of knitting stitch holders they are ideal for the small number of stitches used in crochet.

SCISSORS

Small scissors with sharp points are best as these allow you to isolate one strand of yarn for cutting at a time. Tie a piece of ribbon or yarn to the handle and tie the scissors on your knitting bag to avoid them getting lost.

WOOL SEWING NEEDLES

There are many different sizes of wool sewing needles. Buy those with a big enough eye through which to thread the yarn.

TAPE MEASURE

Use a cloth measure rather than the inflexible metal ones. Most have metric on one side and imperial on the other.

BUTTONS

Adding buttons is a really fantastic way to decorate and finish off a crocheted garment, cushion or accessory. However, always choose your buttons wisely. A cheap unattractive button can undermine the quality of your garment. Make sure you choose the right size button for the buttonhole instructions in the pattern.

Buttons come in all shapes and sizes and are made from many different materials: ceramic, glass, plastic, shell, metal, wood and horn. Check the washing instructions for the buttons as unprotected metal ones may rust.

Try making some crochet buttons (see page 131). These are simple to make and will match your garment perfectly.

✶ Tension

The 'tension' isn't how bad you feel when your crochet has gone wrong, but how tightly or loosely you make the crochet loops.

To make sure that you are working with the measurements that are instructed in the pattern you'll need to make a crocheted tension square. This is because the size of the stitch will vary from person to person – almost everyone works with a different tension. So if you don't work out your tension before you start your pattern, your work may turn out bigger or smaller than you anticipated.

Most patterns follow the tension rule that the stitch size is measured over an area of 10cm (4in) square, counting both rows and stitches.

Crochet through the decades

Tension square

To make a tension square, create a piece of crochet approximately 12.5cm (5in) square using the recommended yarn and stitches in the pattern. Then count the number of rows and the number of stitches over a 10cm (4in) measurement. If these are consistent with the quoted dimensions for this measurement, then your tension has matched the pattern, so you can then use the recommended hook size. If, however, you have more stitches in your square than stated you will need to change to a smaller sized hook. If you have too few stitches, you will need to change to a larger hook to achieve the correct tension.

What you need. . . and what to do with it

★ Crochet – first steps

The first stage of crochet is to find a way of holding the yarn and hook in a comfortable position so that the yarn slips through your fingers. You also need to get the right amount of tension so that you can hold the yarn with your hook as it slips through the loops.

Holding the hook

There are two commonly used ways of holding the hook:

VERSION 1
Pick up the hook and hold it in the same way as a pen (1).

VERSION 2
Pick up the hook and hold it in the same way as a knife (2).

Holding the yarn

You need to hold the yarn so that it slips through your fingers. Here are two commonly used methods:

VERSION 1
Holding the yarn in your right hand, with your left-hand palm facing towards you, hook the yarn with your little finger (3). Turn your hand, catching the yarn with your index finger (4). Your left hand is now free to hold the yarn and hold the crocheted piece of fabric in place. Hold the crochet hook in the right hand (5).

VERSION 2
Holding the yarn in your right hand, with your left-hand palm facing towards you, hook the yarn over the little finger of your left hand, under the ring finger, and over the middle and second finger (6). Your left hand is now free to hold the yarn and hold the crocheted piece of fabric in place. Hold the crochet hook in the right hand (7).

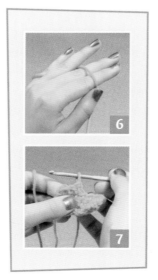

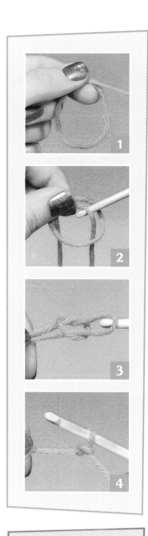

⋆ Stitches

Making the first loop

To make your first loop in crochet, you need to make a slip loop.

To do this, pick up your hook and position the yarn as explained on page 113. Make a loop with the end tail of the yarn (1). Let the tail end drop down over the back of the loop, catch the tail of the yarn with the hook and pull it through the loop (2). Hold the tail end and the ball end of the yarn in your left hand and tighten the loop with the hook in the opposite direction to create a stitch (3). Tighten the loop until it sits comfortably around the hook (4).

Foundation chain (ch)

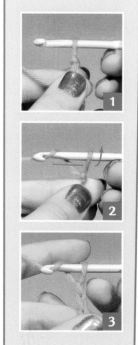

A foundation chain is the basis of all crochet. It's used to begin a crochet pattern, at the beginning of a row and for lace patterns. Your crochet pattern will always tell you how many chains to make. Take care not to make the chains too tight and if you are a beginner be sure to practise your chain until you feel comfortable sliding the hook and yarn through each loop.

With your left hand hold the tail of the slip loop firmly (1). Catch the yarn with the hook and draw it through the loop (2). This makes your first chain. Make as many chains as indicated on the pattern (3). When counting the length of the chain, count each loop but not the one on the hook.

What you need... and what to do with it

Slip stitch/single crochet (ss/sc)

This stitch is more commonly used to join the beginning of a round. If used row after row it creates a very dense, tight piece of fabric.

Make a foundation chain (ch). Holding the end of the chain firmly, insert the hook through the second chain from the hook. Catch the yarn with the hook (a term called 'wrap yarn round hook' – abbreviated as yrh) and pull it through the chain and loop on the hook (1). This leaves one loop on the hook and completes the first slip stitch (ss). Work the next slip stitch into the next chain in the same way. Continue working one ss into each chain until you reach the end of the row. At the end of the row, turn your work, make one chain and continue back along the row in the same way.

Double crochet (dc)

Double crochet is the most common of all crochet stitches. This stitch creates a dense, hard-wearing fabric (see below).

ROW 1
Make a chain. Hold the smooth side of the chain facing you. From front to back, insert the hook through the second chain from the hook (1). There should be two loops on the hook. Wrap the yarn around the hook (yoh or yrh) and pull the yarn through two loops (2). This completes your first double crochet. You should now have one loop on the hook (3). Insert the hook into the next chain and continue until the end of the row, or as the pattern instructs.

ROW 2
When you get to the end of the row, turn your work so that your loop on the hook is at the right edge. In order to start the next row you then need to add a number of chain stitches called 'turning chains'. This will bring your work to the correct height for the next row.

For a double crochet you need one turning chain at the beginning of your row. Pull the loop through the loop on the hook to form a loose chain. This stitch is your first stitch and is counted as the first double crochet. Insert the hook into the next stitch and continue to work one dc into each stitch until the end of the row.

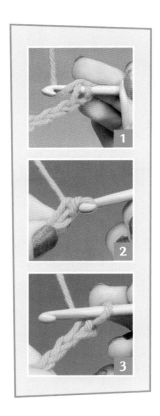

Treble (tr)

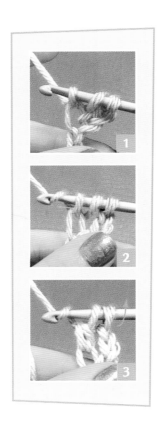

Treble is a taller stitch than double crochet. It also creates a lighter stitch (see below right). It is worked in the same way as a double crochet except the yarn is wrapped around the hook before beginning a stitch. The treble row always starts each row with three chains.

ROW 1

Make a length of chains (ch). Begin the first row by working into the fourth chain from the hook. Wrap yarn around hook (yrh) and draw the yarn through the chain. There are now three loops around the hook (1). Wrap the yarn around the hook and draw yarn through the first two loops on the hook (2). Wrap the yarn around the hook and draw the yarn through the remaining two loops on the hook (3). One loop then remains on the hook. Work a treble into each stitch to the end. Turn and make three turning chains (ch). Work the first treble into the top of the next stitch.

Half treble (htr)

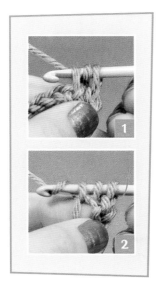

A half treble is slightly shorter than a treble. It is made in a similar way to a double crochet, but with an extra twist of yarn.

Make a length of foundation chains (ch). Wrap the yarn around the hook (yrh) and insert the hook into the third chain from the hook. Draw the yarn through the first loop, leaving three loops on the hook (1). Wrap the yarn round the hook (yrh) again and draw through all three loops on the hook (2).

  What you need… and what to do with it

Double treble (dtr)

Make a length of chains (ch). Wrap the yarn twice around the hook (1), insert the hook in the fifth chain from the hook. Draw the loop through the chain. You now have four loops on the hook (2). Wrap the yarn again and draw through the first two loops (3). Wrap the yarn again (yrh) and draw through the next two loops (4). Wrap the yarn again (yrh) and draw through the last two loops, leaving one loop on the hook (5).

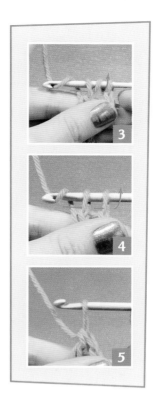

★ Stitch variations

Most stitches are variations of the basic stitches. Once you've practised on a couple of easy projects, moving on to a variation is easy.

Working into a chain space (ch sp)

Insert the hook into the space between the stitches (1).

Clusters (cl)

A cluster is a group of stitches that are joined closely together to give a particular shape. To make a three-treble cluster (3trcl) use the instructions that follow.

Wrap the yarn round the hook (yrh), insert the hook into the stitch, yrh and draw through to the front, yrh and draw through two loops (two loops remain on the hook) (2). Yrh, insert hook into the next stitch, draw through to the front yrh and draw through two loops (three loops remain on the hook) (3). Repeat step 2. There will now be four loops remaining on the hook (4). Yrh and pull through all four loops (5). This completes your three-treble cluster (3trcl).

Popcorns

A variation of a cluster, a popcorn is a group of complete stitches worked into the same place, which is then folded and closed at the top. The number of stitches often varies and will be specified in the pattern. The instructions that follow show how to make a four-treble popcorn.

Make four trebles (tr) into the same place (1). Slip the last loop off the hook and reinsert the hook under the top two loops of the first treble in the group just made and pick up the loop that you took off the hook (2). Pull the loop through to close up the group of stitches (3).

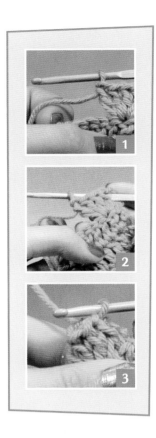

1970s

Crochet through the decades

What you need... and what to do with it

★ Basic techniques

Working in rows

Having finished your foundation chain (ch), you can then begin working in rows. Begin the first row by inserting the hook in either the first, second, third, fourth or fifth chain, depending on the height of the stitch you are using. For example, when working with treble crochet (tr) you need to make three more chains than required in the foundation row and then make the first stitch into the third chain from the hook (1).

This requirement will usually be explained in the pattern. Every following row will begin by using a 'turning chain' (see below) which will bring the stitches up to the height of the stitch you are using and will be counted as your first stitch. The requirements of more complicated stitch patterns vary and will always be instructed in the crochet pattern.

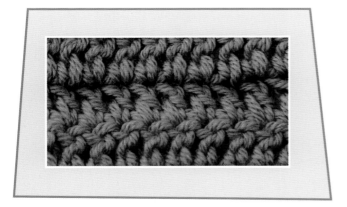

TABLE OF TURNING CHAINS

Double crochet (dc)	1 chain
Half treble (htr)	2 chains
Treble (tr)	3 chains
Double treble (dtr)	4 chains
Triple treble (trtr)	5 chains

Turning the work

When the first row is complete, you will need to turn the work. The trick to keeping a neat edge is to keep the direction you turn in consistent, either clockwise or anti-clockwise. Its easier to find the chain for the next row if you turn your work clockwise.

Working in rounds

One of the pleasures of crochet is that you can create circular constructions without any joining requirements. The basic technique of working in rounds is almost always the same. The thickness of the yarn will determine how many chains you need to make. Your pattern will instruct. To avoid creating too large a hole in the middle of the crochet, you'll usually be instructed to make four or six chains. The sequence that follows starts with six chains. Having created six foundation chains (ch), insert the hook through the first chain. Wrap the yarn around the hook (yrh) and pull the loop through the chain and the loop on the hook (slip stitch). This will make a ring of chains (1). The next stage is usually to work a double crochet (dc) into the ring. Make one chain (2). Then insert the hook into the ring (not into the chain stitch), and make as many double crochets (dc) as the pattern instructs (3).

Marking the round when making spirals

When crocheting in circles you need to make a mark so you know when you've finished your row – otherwise you'll keep going round and round and not know what stage you have reached on your pattern.

Take a short length of yarn in a different colour to your work. Place it over your crochet from front to back, under and to the left of the yarn (1). The yarn will be caught in position under the top of the first stitch. At the end of the round, pull it out and place in position for the next round.

What you need... and what to do with it

Making a square

Make 6ch, ss into first ch to form a ring. Make 3ch, work 2tr into centre of ring. *Make 3 ch, 3tr into centre of ring*, repeat from * to * twice more. Work 3ch. Join with a ss into top of first 3ch to complete the square.

Joining in new yarn and changing colours

If the ball of yarn that you're using runs out or you want to introduce another colour, you'll have to join in the new yarn.

If using double crochet, insert the hook as normal into the stitch using the original yarn and pull a loop through. Drop the old yarn and pick up the new yarn. Wrap new yarn round hook (1) and pull it through the two loops on the hook, in this way completing the double crochet.

When using other stitches, join in same way, introducing new yarn on the last loop of the stitch. Try not to run out of yarn in the middle of a row. If you think you haven't enough yarn to complete the next row, join in new yarn at the beginning of the row to create a neater piece of work that's easier to handle. Work ends of both old and new yarn over a couple of stitches and with scissors cut off the ends of both yarns to create a neat finish (2).

Increasing

Simple increasing means working a number of stitches into the same space. Increases can be made at the edges or at any point along a row or a round.

IN THE MIDDLE OF A ROW

Work one stitch as usual and then make another stitch in the same space as the previous stitch (1). Mark the position of the additional stitch with a contrasting colour or a safety pin to show the placement of the increase for subsequent increases (2).

AT THE END OF A ROW

Work the turning chain as usual. For double crochet and half treble, work two stitches in the first stitch of the previous row. Continue along the row and increase where it is indicated in the pattern (3). For all taller stitches, remember that the turning chain counts as a first stitch, so for those stitches work on one extra stitch in the first stitch of the previous row. The edge will slant outwards.

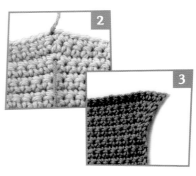

Decreasing

Decreasing is used to make the size of the work smaller. You can decrease in the middle of the work or at the edges. It is most frequently done at the edges to shape a garment, at the underarm seams or around the neck.

AT THE BEGINNING OF A ROW

Add chains for a turning chain, miss a stitch, work a stitch in the next stitch and work across the row to the last two stitches.

AT THE END OF A ROW

Miss the next-to-last stitch and work a stitch in the last stitch.

IN THE MIDDLE OF A ROW

Miss a stitch and work the next stitch. Mark the beginning of the point of decrease with a contrasting colour yarn or a safety pin to show where consequent increases should be.

DECREASING A TREBLE

Yrh, insert hook into top of next st, pull yarn through. Insert hook into top of next st, pull yarn through. Yrh, pull through 3sts, yrh, pull through last two sts (makes 1 decrease).

Fastening off/finishing

Although you only have one stitch to work on at once, you will need to fasten off so that your work doesn't unravel.

Cut your yarn leaving approximately a 15cm (6in) tail. Pull the tail through the loop on the hook and pull tightly (1).

Weaving/sewing in ends

Thread the yarn with a wool sewing needle or a blunt-ended needle with a large enough eye for the size of the yarn or thread.

Weave the needle in and out of stitches near the cast off edge and pull the yarn through (1). Cut off end neatly with a sharp pair of scissors.

  What you need... and what to do with it

★ How to read a crochet pattern

Reading a crochet pattern is something that puts many people off. The terminology can look very daunting and in this book I have tried to keep it as simple as possible and have included explanations in full where necessary.

Patterns are usually laid out in the same way, first showing the materials needed to make the item. Then giving you the brand name of the yarn with the shade numbers and the amount you'll need. If it is a garment there will be a different amount of yarn given for each size. A pattern will also give you the hook size you need and details of any other accessories. You will then be taken through a step-by-step, row-by-row instruction. Crochet uses abbreviations which will be listed with an explanation of what each one means.

The instructions are there to make the patterns make good, clear sense and should follow a logical pattern. For example '1dc in next st' means work one double crochet stitch in the next stitch in the row below. If you are an absolute beginner, it will become clear once you have worked through the 'What You Need… And What To Do With It' section.

A pattern repeat can be given in several ways, the most usual is shown using an asterisk. For example: *3tr, 3ch, miss 3sts, rep from * to last 3sts. This means that you repeat the stitches instructed between the asterisks until you get to the end of the row, where you'll have 3sts left at the end and you'll be instructed to work according to the pattern. Another way to explain repeats is by putting the instruction into a bracket: (3tr, 3ch, miss 3sts) four times. This means repeat the instruction that is within the bracket four times.

If the pattern states 'right side' or RS, make sure you mark it. A piece of crochet has no 'right' or 'wrong' side until it is given one, either because a stitch with a texture has been included or two pieces of yarn have been joined together leaving a tail on one side.

UK and US terminology differs considerably in crochet. It seems that in the UK stitches are named after the number of loops on the hook *including* the first loop (see page 114) while in the US it *excludes* that loop. The chart below explains the differences in the descriptions of the stitches. The terminology

DIFFERENCES IN COMMON CROCHET TERMINOLOGY

United Kingdom	United States
Slip stitch (ss)	Slip stitch (sl st)
Double crochet (dc)	Single crochet (sc)
Half treble (htr)	Half double crochet (hdc)
Treble (tr)	Double crochet (dc)
Double treble (dtr)	Treble (tr)
Triple treble (trtr)	Double treble (dtr)
Quadruple treble (quadtr)	Triple treble or Long treble (trtr)
Tunisian stitch	Afghan stitch
Miss	Skip
Tension	Gauge

✳ Crochet beading

Thread the beads onto the yarn before you start to crochet.
If the bead holes are too small for the ryr of the needle to go
through the eye of the needle use the following threading
method:

Double thread a sewing needle (1). Loop the yarn through
it and draw the bead over the needle over the thin cotton and
onto the yarn (2). Always bead on a wrong-side row and
place the bead to the back of the work.

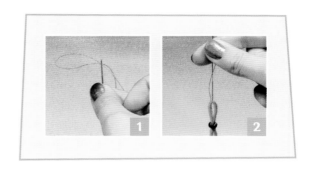

Beading on double crochet

Insert hook, wrap yarn around the hook
(yrh), pull loop through, slide bead up yarn
and place it close to the work (1).
Yrh, (catch yarn beyond bead), pull
through both loops on hook (2).

Beading on trebles

Wrap yarn round the hook (yrh), insert
hook, yrh and pull the two loops through.
Slide a bead up the yarn and place it close

to the work. Yrh (catch yarn beyond bead),
and pull through both loops on hook.
Continue with pattern instructions.

✳ Seams

When joining crochet pieces make sure they are the correct size.
Try and join motifs as they are being made and choose the type
of seam that best suits the item and the yarn or thread. Use the

same yarn or thread that is in the crochet, unless the yarn is
particularly bulky or chunky. In this case you should use a finer
matching yarn to prevent the seams from bunching up.

Back stitch seam

This is a hard-wearing seam, ideal for items such as bags and for areas of clothing where strength is an advantage, such as shoulder seams.

With the wrong side facing and the right sides together, match the stitches or rows. Using a wool sewing needle or needle with a big enough eye for the yarn or thread, sew in back stitch (1).

Woven seam

This is a flatter seam, suitable for finer pieces of crochet work.

Lay the pieces with the edges touching and the wrong side facing up. Then use a wool or tapestry sewing needle and weave around the centres of the edge stitches (2). Take care not to pull the stitches too tightly.

Slip stitch seam

This seam can be worked with the right sides together so the ridge of the seam is inside the work, or with the wrong sides together so that the ridge is shown on the right side of the work.

Put the hook into each corresponding stitch of each edge and work one slip stitch through each pair of stitches along the seam (3).

Double crochet seam

Sewing together crochet with double crochet is another simple way to join a seam. It can leave a ridge. This can either be used as a feature on the right side, or the seam can be double crocheted on the wrong side and then turned to reveal an invisible seam on the right side.

Insert the hook in each of the corresponding stitches along the seam and double crochet into each stitch until the end (4).

★ Edgings

Edgings are the perfect way to make a garment look finished and professional. Knitted or crocheted garments can be livened up by a crocheted edging and they are easy to add on. Four easy edgings are explained below and opposite. Always start by making one row of double crochet to set the edging off. If using one colour, continue as follows. If using a different colour for the edging, join yarn by using a ss.

Double crochet edging

Make 1ch. Insert the hook into each stitch along the row or round.

You will often need 3dc in each corner stitch otherwise work will not lie flat.

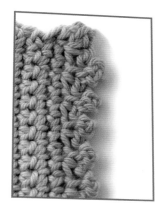

Picot edging

Join yarn by using ss.

ROW 1
1dc into each st, turn.

ROW 2
1dc *3ch, ss into third ch from hook, miss 1st, 1dc into next st; rep from * to end.

Shell edging

Join yarn by using ss.

ROW 1
1dc into each st, turn.

ROW 2
1dc *miss 1 st, 5tr into next st, miss 1st, 1dc into next st; rep from * to end.

Frill edging

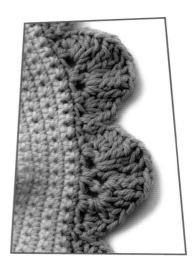

The pattern for this stitch works in sections of eight stitches. So you need enough stitches so the total will divide equally by eight.

ROW 1

1dc into each st, turn.

ROW 2

*1ch, miss 1st, 1dc 1ch 1htr in next st, miss 1st, 1tr 1ch 1tr in next st, miss 1st, 1htr 1ch 1dc in next st, 1ch, miss 1st, 1ss in next st, rep from * to end placing the last ss in beginning of row. Turn 1ch.

ROW 3

*1dc, 1htr in next ch sp, 3tr in next ch sp, 3dtr 1ch 3dtr in next ch sp, 3tr in next ch sp, 1htr 1dc in next ch sp, 1ss on ss, rep from * to end. Fasten off.

Crochet through the decades

★ Embellishments

Pom-poms, tassels, flowers, fringes and crocheted buttons are all ways to make your crochet individual and unique. These easily made embellishments can make all the difference to a simple piece of fabric and turn it into something quite beautiful. Using the following instructions for different embellishments, try using up oddments of yarn or balancing the main fabric with a differently textured yarn. In the pom-poms we added a few strands of lurex and a thick slub yarn, which gave them a rich texture.

What you need... and what to do with it

Pom-poms

Pom-poms can liven up a cushion, throw, hat, scarf or hot-water bottle cover. Try using strands of yarn in different colours to make multi-coloured ones. When you have used up one colour, just change to a different colour.

Cut out two circles of card (an empty cereal packet will do nicely) to the size you want your pom-pom to be, using a cup or other circular utensil as a guide (1). Cut a small hole in the centre of each circle (2). Place the two circles together. Wind some wool off a ball to make a small ball. Put the tail through the small circle and start winding it round the card and through the hole (3), until the hole is so small that you can't get any more wool through. For a thinner pom-pom, use less wool. When the last piece of yarn is used up, pull the yarn apart at the outer circle with both index fingers to reveal the card. Insert scissors between the two pieces of card. Holding the tail of yarn with your left hand, cut round the outer edge of the pom-pom (4). When you have cut all the way round, wind a separate piece of yarn between the two pieces of card. Secure very tightly in a double knot (5). Remove the two cards and trim the pom-pom.

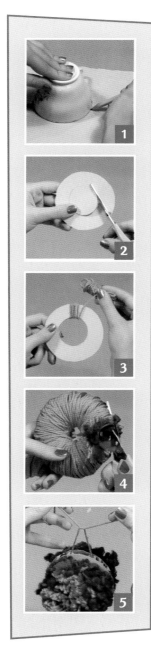

Mini pom-poms

If you want to make a mini pom-pom, the hole in the above method will be too small to push the yarn through. Here is a quick and easy method for making a mini pom-pom.

Wrap the yarn around two fingers 70 or 80 times. Slide the yarn bunch off your fingers and, holding on to one end of the bunch, pick up the yarn and wrap it around the centre of the bunch tightly. Cut the yarn leaving a 25cm (10in) tail. Thread the yarn through a wool sewing needle and push the needle through the centre where the yarn has been wrapped three or four times, then wrap the yarn around and push the needle through the centre again so that it's wrapped very tightly. Break the yarn. Take some sharp scissors and cut through the loops at both ends. Fluff out the pom-pom and trim the ends to make an even sphere. To make the pom pom look very fluffy and dense, don't be afraid to cut it down quite severely.

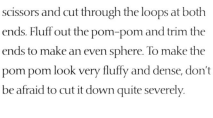

Tassels

Find a cassette or CD case, or anything solid that is the required tassel length. Wrap wool round the object 30–40 times, depending on the thickness of the wool and how fat you want the tassel (1 and 2). Take another piece of yarn and thread it through the top of the wool on the object. Tie very tight with a double knot. Then pull all the wool off. Holding the top of the tassel with your left hand, cut the bottom to form tassels (3). Then cut a separate piece of yarn. Tie the yarn around the tassel and make a neck, wrapping the yarn around the tassel several times. Secure with a double knot (4). Thread the same piece of yarn with a sewing needle and push the needle from front to back several times to secure. Trim the bottom.

Fringes

Find a cassette or CD case, or anything solid that is the required length of the fringe. Wrap wool round the object four or five times, depending on the thickness of the wool and how fat you want the fringe (1). Slide the yarn off, holding it tightly at the top. Push the fringe up through the bottom loop of the item, using either your fingers or a crochet hook (2). Making a loop with the fringe, push the bottom of the tassel though it and pull tight (3). Trim the bottom strands.

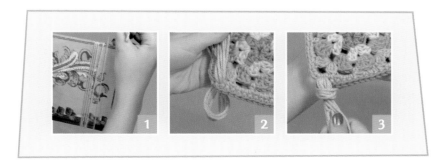

What you need… and what to do with it

Little flower

Make 6ch, ss into first ch to form a ring.

ROUND 1

1ch, work 15dc into ring, ss into first dc.

ROUND 2

*3ch, tr2tog as follows over next 2sts.
Yrh, insert hook into next st, yrh and pull through. Yrh, pull through two loops (leaving two loops on hook). Yrh, insert hook into next st and pull through. Yrh, pull through two loops, yrh and pull through all three loops. Ss into next dc*. Repeat from * to * four times making five petals, placing last ss into last dc of previous round. Fasten off.

Pierrot button

Make 3ch, join ring with 1ss.

ROUND 1

3ch, 12tr into centre of ring, join with 1ss to top of 3ch.

ROUND 2

1ch, 1dc in each tr, 1ss to join.

ROUND 3

As Round 2.
Leave a long end, approx 20cm (8in). Using a tapestry needle, weave the end through the stitches. Cut some of the same yarn off the ball and fill the centre of the button very firmly. Using the loose end of the yarn, draw the stitches tightly together. Fasten off and use the same thread to attach the button to your item.

Two-colour button

Make 3ch, form a ring with 1ss.

ROUND 1

1ch, 5dc into ring with first colour. Fasten off.

ROUND 2

Using second colour, 3ch, 1tr in same st, 2tr into each dc to end. Join with 1ss. Thread a 20cm (8in) yarn end through each st and finish by filling the centre of the button firmly with yarn from same ball. Using the loose end of the yarn, draw the stitches tightly together. Fasten off.

★ Where to buy yarn and cottons

If you are under the impression that the only yarn available is the itchy woollen stuff, or the acrylic type that makes your hair stand on end, then think again. The new yarns that have taken over the high street are soft, fleecy, sometimes wacky, and in textures and colours beyond your wildest yarn dreams.

Wool is no longer something you have to buy to make cheap clothes for your family; it can now be regarded as an exotic textile, a piece of art, something to satisfy your senses. It's worth searching around for yarns just to discover the textures and the new sumptuous colours available.

INTERNET YARN SUPPLIERS

Probably the best places to source your yarn are Internet yarn suppliers, and more and more people are now following this trend and shopping online. These suppliers often have a much wider range to offer than traditional high-street shops and will mail directly to your door. Make sure you find an Internet company that has a good range of photographs of the yarn and the patterns available, and offers you the option to return any yarn that doesn't live up to expectations. It can be a real pleasure shopping for wool online, especially when you receive your parcel full of crochet goodies – it's just like having a present delivered through the post.

DEPARTMENT STORES

Supplies can be limited through department stores, but with the new popularity in crafts in general, stores are beginning to expand their yarn ranges.

HIGH-STREET WOOL STORES

The small wool and haberdashery shops of old have mostly closed down. There is, however, a new wave of high-street wool shops that are emerging: they're spacious, open-plan, and sometimes have an area for cappuccinos. Often they offer workshops in crochet and knitting.

CHARITY STORES

The tradition of unravelling a garment and reusing the wool to make something new still has a valid place, so if you're trying to crochet on a tight budget, go along to your local charity store where you can nearly always find something hand-knitted or crocheted. It's also a good place to unearth yarns and cottons that people have never used, those that have been hoarded in lofts for years.

Wherever possible, try to use the brand and type of yarn specified in the pattern. However, yarns can also be substituted, in which case you should match the weight and length of the substitute yarn. Also check the hook size that is recommended in the pattern as this can give you a general guide to the yarn thickness and enable you to find a substitute. Always make a tension square (see page 112) and adjust your needle size accordingly.

⭐ Carrying and storing yarn and crochet

A PORTABLE CRAFT

Crochet is one of the most portable crafts. Unlike knitting, which requires two pointed needles, crochet has only one small hook that can easily pop inside a neat little bag, ready to be whipped out and used at the earliest opportunity. There is also only one stitch, so if it slips off the hook for any reason you only have one stitch to pick up.

Crochet is often worked in small patchwork squares and then sewn together, so projects are usually easy to carry around.

STORING YARN

The luscious colours and sumptuous feel of merino, alpaca, cashmere, angora and fancy yarns look so appealing that people buy them solely as a stylish interior feature that can be displayed proudly in a basket within a room. The colours that are popular in yarn now tend to match the National Trust and other designer paint palettes and no longer have to be hidden in the loft to waste away.

However, if you decide you have so much spare yarn that you need to put some away safely, make sure the yarn is stored in a dry area. Plastic boxes with lids are useful, or alternatively put the yarn in a plastic bag inside a basket or box. The last thing you want is mice getting hold of your precious fibre, or the cat infesting it with fleas.

STORING HOOKS

Hooks are small things and, like ballpoint pens, tend to get lost. Find an attractive pot to keep them in for easy access.

Washing, blocking and steaming

Washing

Creating your own piece of crochet takes considerable time and trouble and the last thing you want is to ruin your work by washing it incorrectly.

Yarn labels usually have international labelling standards for their care. Most yarns can be successfully cleaned by careful hand washing. Check the label and if the yarn can be machine washed make sure you set the machine to the recommended temperature.

General hand-washing instructions

* Use soap flakes that are recommended for hand washing and dissolve them in the water before immersing your garment. Make sure the water is only hand hot.
* Rinse the garment twice in cooler water.
* Give the garment a short spin in the machine, or if the item is very delicate place it in a towel and gently squeeze out the excess moisture.
* Work the garment carefully into shape and place on a dry towel on a flat surface, or a dry towel hung over a clothes horse or on a clothes line to dry.

Machine washing

The label should give the recommended temperature at which to set the machine. General temperature guidelines:

60°C/140°F – too hot to the touch
50°C/120°F – hand hot
40°C/104°F – warm to the touch
30° C/86°F – cool

Washing special yarns

* Lightweight and mercerized cottons are best washed by hand.
* Heavyweight cottons are fine to wash in the machine on a cool wash, and should then be dried flat.
* Fancy yarns, such as lurex, mohair and chenille, can be dry cleaned – check the labels.
* Leather, string, raffia and sisal constructions should be wiped down with a cloth or sponge and left to dry.

Pressing

Pressing your crocheted fabric can make the difference between it looking like a professional piece of art or an old rag. Yarn with a high content of natural fibre can be pressed, but some yarn can be totally ruined by a hot iron. Check the label for the pressing instructions – it should give you all the help you need, other than switching the iron on for you! Yarn labels are very useful for telling you at which temperature to set the iron, or whether you need a damp or a dry cloth.

1990s

Crochet through the decades

Damp finishing

If you are instructed that the yarn is not to be pressed, then follow the instructions below:

First of all find a colourfast towel and then make it damp. The next stage is to lie the towel flat, lay your pieces of fabric on the towel and roll them up together loosely. Leave like this for approximately one hour so that the crocheted piece absorbs the dampness from the towel.

Undo the towel on a flat surface and place the pieces once more on top of it. Pin the pieces into shape with pins (blocking). Find another damp cloth or towel and lay it over the top so your fabric is sandwiched. Press gently down onto your fabric so every part of it is touching the cloth and leave it to dry in a place that is not going to stay damp for too long, or it will smell musty – an airing cupboard is ideal.

Blocking

This is a method used to keep your garment in shape while it is drying. It is also used as a method to pin a garment out into shape before sewing it up, especially for any pieces that tend to curl up at the edges.

After washing and when the fabric has had the moisture squeezed out and is still damp, shape it into position on a dry towel ideally placed on a padded surface. Ease the fabric into place, right side facing upwards, to achieve the correct measurements. Then pin out the pieces using large-headed coloured pins (this is where the padding comes into its own). Make a point of placing the pins on the very outer edges of the fabric.

PART THREE

Patterns...

... to get you hooked

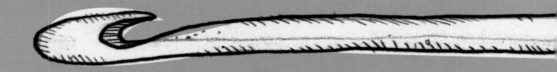

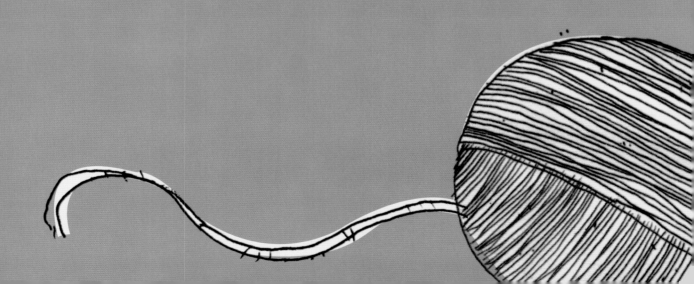

The yarn starts here...

Crochet trends have changed dramatically in recent years and in the 20 patterns that follow the yarns, designs and crochet pieces have been chosen to represent the new and stylish ways of using this absorbing and versatile craft. Crochet was traditionally associated with fine threads and intricate work using hooks often little bigger than a tapestry needle. But in the late 20th century the abundance of thicker, natural and creatively mixed yarns in the marketplace hailed an upsurge in the popularity of crochet. The craft is all around us – just look in the fashion pages of consumer magazines and supplements, as well as on the fashion catwalks, to find crocheted inspiration. Every one of these patterns is designed to be as simple as possible so that beginners will feel comfortable and unthreatened by any complicated stitches, but the items are all so tempting that even the seasoned, or lapsed crocheter will be lured towards picking up the hook again.

When deciding what to crochet, many people want to make something special for their home, so with this in mind there are two beautiful patterns for cushions; one round (see the Cushion Cake on page 178) and one square (see the Loopy Cushion on page 181). They both have an individuality that can be adapted by changing the colour scheme to suit any décor. The cushions use Rooster Aran yarn, which come in a mix of alpaca and pure wool and are perfect for snuggling up to at the end of the sofa. The Flower Throw on page 142 is made up of simple squares and is soft, luxurious and made in beautiful colours. The squares make it a perfect ongoing project as you can work on one or two squares in an evening and then put your work down until you feel like starting again. As opposed to knitting, where the dropped stitches on half-finished work can drive the knitter to distraction, crochet only ever has one loop on the hook at a time so you don't lose your stitches when you put it down. And then when you go to bed, why not curl up with the warm and toasty Hot-Water bottle Cover with pom-pom ties (see page 176). Made using Rowan Big wool, a thick superchunky wool that is quick and easy to work with, this can be made in one evening – especially when the temperature plummets!

Bolero and wrap-over cardigans are elegant and fashionable and we've combined both into one garment – the Tie Bolero Cardigan on page 157 can be tied at the front, or wrapped around and tied at the back or on the side. It uses Debbie Bliss Baby Cashmerino yarn, a soft, light yarn that shows the stitch detail without being bulky. The same yarn is used to make the Daisy Cashmere Scarf on page 167, made with simple squares decorated with little pom-poms instead of the traditional fringe. This scarf can also be combined with the elegant Fingerless Gloves with lace edgings shown on page 170. Made using Debbie Bliss Alpaca Silk, these feel so glorious to wear that you won't ever want to take them off!

It seems that many people nowadays also want to create their own fashion accessories, so we've included some fantastic items that complement any cool outfit. They are also perfect gifts: homemade gifts are so much nicer and more satisfying than shop-bought gifts. Once made, and presented wrapped in coloured tissue and tied with a ribbon they look as good as anything you can buy commercially.

Ribbon and flowers have been used in many of the patterns: a simple crochet flower or a piece of ribbon enables the transformation of a plain-looking garment or accessory into something quite individual. The Flower-Power Beaded Belt on page 162 combines beads, flowers and ribbon, providing the perfect accessory for a light summer skirt and just as effective threaded through the belt loops of a denim skirt or jeans.

The Beanie Hats on page 140 went down so well that we made loads of them in different colours. This simple design uses basic stitches and is a good introduction to shaping techniques. Our other hat is a very pretty Summer Brimmed Hat (see page 164), an ideal strategy for keeping the sun off with style. The Ribbon Slippers on page 174 are quite divine – they are so cute and come in three different sizes and you may find that your friends and family will be begging you to make some for them. The glamorous Frill Shawl on page 144 is made using a fine mohair yarn called Rowan Kid Silk Haze, which comes in an impressive range of elegant colours. The popular teal shade is shown as the main colour, edged with the addition of a frill in rose pink that sways and swishes and makes the wearer feel like Marilyn Monroe.

There are two crochet bag patterns. One of them is a delicate Beaded Purse (see page 173), which is a very pretty accessory for a little evening number when just a minimum of items needs to be carried. The Mesh Bag (see page 154) is bright, colourful and funky, made using Colinette Point Five chunky yarn and a double knit cotton. This bag makes a definite fashion statement and is for girls who want to make a strong impression.

Finally we come to our pets – and how could we possibly forget about them! Marley, our model puppy, couldn't believe his luck when we designed and made a Stripy Dog Blanket especially for him (see page 150). The stripes hide the dog hairs and muddy paws and the blanket is made using the fabulous Rooster Aran yarn. We used each of the Rooster Aran range of colours which make a perfect matching colour palette. The blanket can be made in two sizes – large and small – depending on the size of your puppy. This blanket has the added flexibility that you can use any type of yarn and work it to any size, as it has no shaping – and it's made using a simple half treble stitch. If I were less of a pet lover I would say it was too good to be a pet blanket. We have equally spoiled Pebbles the cat, a rather funky cat that well suits the Pet's Playmat on page 146. The cosy mat is made in the round so Pebbles doesn't have to look round corners for his prey, and has a swishy tasselled edge that he can play with when the mice are sleeping.

The designers involved with creating the patterns included here are principally young design experts working in the textile industry with fresh new ideas to bring to the newly revived craft of crochet. The final range of uplifting patterns that we have selected for this book is testimony to the endurance of a craft that has proved itself able to switch and change according to current trends. Crochet has once again emerged from its hidden cocoon to demonstrate its adaptability and its beauty – a craft that now represents the essence of cool.

2000s

Crochet through the decades

  Patterns... to get you hooked

Abbreviations

ch	*chain*	alt	*alternate*
ss	*slip stitch*	approx	*approximately*
dc	*double crochet*	beg	*beginning*
dtr	*double treble*	ch sp	*chain space*
htr	*half treble*	cc	*contrasting colour*
qtr	*quadruple treble*	cont	*continue*
tr	*tr*	dec	*decrease*
trtr	*triple treble*	foll	*following*
		in	*inch(es)*
		inc	*increase*
		lp(s)	*loop(s)*
		m	*metre(s)*
		MC	*main colour*
		mm	*millimetre(s)*
		patt(s)	*pattern(s)*
		rem	*remain*
		rep	*repeat*
		RS	*right side*
		sp(s)	*space(s)*
		st(s)	*stitch(es)*
		t-ch	*turning chain*
		tog	*together*
		WS	*wrong side*
		yrh	*wrap yarn around hook*

Beanie hat

This simple beanie hat, made in one size, uses three basic stitches and is an ideal first project. It looks great in any colour, or if you feel ambitious try creating stripes (see page 121 for joining in new yarn). Add a flower or a pom-pom, or change to a textured wool to alter the look completely.

MATERIALS
Rooster Almerino Aran (50g balls)
shade 307, Brighton Rock x 2 balls

Crochet hook: size 4.50mm

STITCHES USED
double crochet, slip stitch, half treble, treble

ABBREVIATIONS

ch chain	dc double crochet
dec decrease	htr half treble
ss slip stitch	tr treble

METHOD
All sts are worked into back loop of dc, htr, tr.

Round 1: Make 90ch, ss into first ch.

Round 2: 1ch (counts as first dc) 1dc into each ch to end. Ss into top of first dc.

Rounds 3–6: Repeat Round 2, four more times.

Round 7: 2ch (counts as 1st htr) 1htr into each dc until end of round. Ss into top of first htr.

Rounds 8–11: Repeat Round 7, four more times.

Round 12: 3ch 1tr into each htr, ss into top of first tr.

Round 13: 3ch (counts as first tr) 6tr, dec 1st (yrh, insert hook into top of next st, pull yarn through, insert hook into top of next st, pull yarn through, yrh, pull through first 3sts, yrh, pull through last 2sts) *7tr, dec 1st*. Repeat from * to * to end. Ss into top of first 3ch.

Round 14: 3ch (counts as 1st tr) 5tr, dec 1st *6tr, dec 1st*. Repeat from * to * to end. Ss into top of first 3ch.

Round 15: 2ch (counts as first htr) 4htr, dec 1st (same as before) *5htr, dec 1st*. Repeat from * to * to end. Ss into top of first 2ch.

Round 16: 2ch (counts as first htr) 3htr, dec 1st *4htr, dec 1st*. Repeat from * to * to end. Ss into top of first 2ch.

Round 17: 2ch (counts as first htr) 2htr, dec 1st *3htr, dec 1st*. Repeat from * to * to end. Ss into top of first 2ch.

Round 18: 3ch (counts as first tr) 1tr, dec 1st *2tr, dec 1st*. Repeat from * to * to end. Ss into top of first 3ch.

Round 19: 3ch (counts as first tr) dec 1st *1tr, dec 1st*. Repeat from * to * to end. Ss into top of first 3ch.

Round 20: 3ch (counts as first tr) 1tr into each tr to end. Ss into top of first 3ch.

To Make Up
With wool sewing needle and 20cm (8in) yarn, weave in and out of top of the last row of treble around top of hat. Hold beginning of yarn and pull together until the hole is closed. Fasten off by making a knot and sew in yarn ends neatly.

Flower blanket

The mixture of colours in this throw complement each other beautifully. The squares are very straightforward; as soon as you've got the hang of one, you just have to do another 59. The throw is a real showpiece in any home.

MEASUREMENTS
Each square measures 16.5 x 16.5cm (6½ x 6½in)
Overall size of throw approximately 99 x 165cm (39 x 65in)

MATERIALS
Rooster Almerino Aran (50g balls)
Yarn A: shade 301, Cornish x 5 balls
Yarn B: shade 302, Sugared Almond x 1 ball
Yarn C: shade 306, Gooseberry x 5 balls
Yarn D: shade 304, Mushroom x 11 balls
Yarn E: shade 303, Strawberry Cream x 1 ball
Yarn F: shade 307, Brighton Rock x 1 ball
Yarn G: shade 305, Custard x 1 ball

Crochet hook: size 6.00mm

STITCHES USED
chain, double crochet, double treble, slip stitch, treble

ABBREVIATIONS
ch chain	ch sp chain space
dc double crochet	dtr double treble
ss slip stitch	tr treble
WS wrong side	

METHOD
All stitches to be worked into back of each st.

Round 1: Using yarn A make 4ch, join with a ss.

Round 2: Into centre of ring make 3dc, 2ch *3dc, 2ch*. Repeat from * to * twice more and join with a ss into top of first dc. Break yarn.

Round 3: Join in colour B, E, F or G (work 15 squares alternating these colours).
Make 6ch *3dtr, 2ch, 3dtr, 2ch into next ch sp (corner)*. Repeat into next two corners. Work 3dtr, 2ch, 2dtr into next corner ch sp, ss into fourth of first 6ch. Break yarn.

Round 4: Join new yarn by putting hook through next ch sp, pull new colour through and ss. 3ch, 2tr into same ch sp, *2ch 3tr 3ch 3tr into next corner (next ch sp). 2ch, 3tr into next ch sp* Repeat from * to * twice more.
2ch, 3tr, 3ch, 3tr into next corner (ch sp).
2ch, ss into top of first 3ch.
Break yarn.

Round 5: Join in yarn A. Make 1ch. Work 1dc into top edge of all stitches of previous row, at each corner work 1dc 1ch 1dc into centre chain. Join with a ss. Break yarn.

Round 6: Join in yarn D. Make 1ch. Work 1dc into top edge of all stitches from previous row, at each corner work 1dc 1ch 1dc into centre chain. Join with ss into first chain.

Round 7: Repeat Round 6.
Break yarn.

Make 15 squares of each petal colour.

To Make Up
Take two squares and hold WS together. Using yarn D join squares with a double crochet seam (see page 125).
Join work in strips vertically and then horizontally.

Edging
Using yarn D, dc in each stitch all the way round; in each corner make 2dc into corner stitch.
Sew in yarn ends neatly.

Frill shawl

This truly elegant garment made with Rowan Kid Silk Haze is light and soft and available in a range of beautiful colours. An excellent beginner's project, this shawl consists mainly of a series of chain stitches. It's made in one size and is crocheted using diamond net stitch edged with a line of double crochet, topped off with a frill edging. Remember to keep your tension fairly loose otherwise it will be tricky picking up the chains when forming the diamond net stitch.

MEASUREMENTS
Approximately 170 x 70cm (67 x 27½in)

MATERIALS
Rowan Kid Silk Haze (25g balls)
Yarn A (main colour): shade 582, Trance x 2 balls
Yarn B (edging): shade 583, Blushes x 2 balls

Crochet hook: size 3.50mm

STITCHES USED
chain, double crochet, slip stitch, double treble

ABBREVIATIONS
ch chain	ch sp chain space
dc double crochet	ss slip stitch
dtr double treble	

METHOD
Make a foundation chain of 140ch, plus 2ch to turn
(the number of chains must be a multiple of 4+2ch).

Row 1: Make 1dc in second chain from hook, *make 5ch, miss 3ch, 1ss in next ch* Repeat from * to * to end. Make 7ch, turn.
Row 2: *Make 1ss in third ch in centre of first 5ch arch, 5ch* repeat from * to * across row ending with 1ss in third ch of last arch, 2ch, work 1dtr in last stitch, 6ch, turn.
Row 3: 1ss in third ch of first 5ch arch. *5ch, 1ss in third ch of next arch* repeat from * to * across 7ch, turn.

Repeat Rows 2 and 3 for the rest of the pattern until you have crocheted 140 rows.

Frill edging
To achieve a neat, professional finish it is always a good idea to start with one row of double crochet to set the edging off. Continue using yarn A to start your edging as follows:

Using yarn A work 1dc in each st across width until corner. Work 3dc into each corner st. Continuing along length, *make 3dc into each ch sp, 1dc into top of next st*. Repeat from * to * until corner. Work 3dc into corner st. Work each width and each length once more. Ss to join. Fasten off.

Sew in yarn ends.

Tip: At this point hold the floating end of yarn parallel with the fabric edge and work your dc over it. This ensures easy finishing, allowing you to confidently snip off the ends knowing that your work will not unravel.

At the beginning of one of the long sides, join using yarn B. Work *20ch, ss into next stitch, work 10ch ss into next stitch* repeat from * to * until you have completely worked the edging all round the piece. Fasten off neatly.

Pet's playmat

This charming round mat is perfect for your pampered pussy cat to frolic on, so he can squeeze in those much-needed hours of kip without dragging himself to the sofa! It is crocheted in a round on a slightly smaller hook than usual to give a firm fabric in which claws are less liable to catch. You can invent colour combinations to suit your cat's personality and your décor, choosing from the luscious Rooster colour palette. When you start you may think the mat is 'frilling', but by the end of Round 6 it should begin to lie flat, and then gets flatter the further out you work.

MATERIALS

Rooster Almerino Aran (50g balls)
Yarn A (main colour): shade 308, Spiced Plum x 2 balls
Yarn B: shade 310, Rooster x 2 balls
Yarn C: shade 307, Brighton Rock x 2 balls
Yarn D: shade 305, Custard x 3 balls

Crochet hook: size 4.50mm

STITCHES USED

double crochet, treble, double treble crochet, slip stitch

ABBREVIATIONS

ch chain
tr treble
ss slip stitch

dc double crochet
dtr double treble

METHOD

Using yarn A make 6ch. Join with a ss in first ch to form a ring.

Round 1: 2ch, make 12dc into middle of circle, ss into second of first 2ch. Do not turn at the end of this round or any throughout the pattern. (12sts)

Round 2: 2ch, make 3dc into next st (make 3dc into next st). Repeat all round the circle, ss into second of first 2ch. (36sts)

Round 3: 2ch, make 3dc into next st, 1dc into each of next 2sts (3dc into next st, 1dc into each of next 2sts). Repeat all round circle. Ss into second of first 2ch.(60sts)

Round 4: (make 5ch, 1dc into fourth st). Repeat all round circle. Ss into first ch (this leaves 15 loops around the outside of circle).

Round 5: 2ch (5dc into space of loop) repeat all round the circle, ss in second of first 2ch. (75sts)

Round 6: 3ch, starting in the next st make 1tr into each of next 9sts, 2tr into next st. (1tr into each of next 8sts, 2tr into next st, 1tr into each of next 9sts. 2tr into next st). Repeat all round circle. 1ss into first 3ch. (84sts)

Round 7: This is where the circle begins to grow evenly and methodically; what you are actually doing is increasing 12sts throughout the round. If you find that the increases are causing the circle to have points, then stagger the increases periodically. 4ch, starting in the next st (these 4ch at the beginning of rounds count as the first dtr). (1dtr into each of next 6sts, 2dtr into next st). Repeat all round circle, 1ss into fourth of first 4ch. (96sts)

Round 8: 4ch, starting in the next st (1dtr into each of next 7sts, 2dtr into next st). Repeat all round circle. Ss into fourth of first 4ch. (108sts)

Round 9: 4ch, starting in the next st (1dtr into each of next 8sts, 2dtr into next st). Repeat all round circle. Ss into fourth of first 4ch. (120sts)

Rounds 10 and 11: Repeat Round 9 twice, making one more dtr between each increase, as is shown in rounds 7 (132sts), round 8 (148sts), round 9. (156sts)

Round 12: Using yarn B, starting in the next st, (1dtr into each of next 11sts, 2dtr into next st). Repeat all round circle. Ss into fourth of first 4ch. (168sts)

Rounds 13, 14, 15, 16: Repeat round 12 four more times, making one more dtr between each increase as is shown in rounds 7, 8 and 9. (226sts)

Rounds 17: Using yarn C, 4ch, starting in the next st (1dtr in each of the next 16sts, 2dtr into next st). Repeat all round circle. Ss into fourth of first 4ch. (238sts)

Rounds 18, 19, 20: Repeat round 17 three more times, making one more dtr between each increase as is shown in rounds 7, 8 and 9. (274sts)

Round 21: Using yarn D, 4ch, starting in the next st (1dtr into each of next 20sts, 2dtr in the next st). Repeat all round circle. Ss into fourth of first 4ch. (268sts)

Round 22: Repeat round 21 once, making one more dtr between each increase as is shown in rounds 7, 8 and 9. (298sts). Fasten off.

Finishing
Neatly sew in ends.
Block gently, shaping into a circle as you work.

To make the fringe

1. Cut a piece of card that is 12 x 20cm (4¾ x 8in).
2. Using yarn D, wrap the yarn completely around the narrower width of the card five times, finishing at the same edge as you started.
3. Cut the yarn along the long edge of the card.
4. Keeping the yarn folded, slip it off the card and with your crochet hook pull the loop of folded yarn through a chain space on the outside of the circle.
5. Catch the long ends of the yarn into the hook and pull them through the loop you have just made.
6. Tug the ends to make a tight knot onto the edge.
7. Repeat this in every other chain around the circle.
8. When fringe is finished, trim and tidy any stray threads around the edge.

Summer flower camisole

This beautiful and feminine camisole goes well with either jeans or an elegant skirt.

MEASUREMENTS

To fit bust 82/87/92cms (32/34/36in)

Actual size 84/89/94cms (33/35/37in)

MATERIALS

(50g balls)

Rowan 4 ply cotton shade 131, Fresh x 5 balls

Rowan Cotton Glacé in the following shades: 811 Tickle; 815 Excite; 747 Candy Floss; 814 Shoot x 1 ball each

Crochet hook: size 2.00mm

TENSION
16sts and 9 rows of pattern to 5cm (2in) on size 2.00mm crochet hook using half treble.

STITCHES USED
half treble, double crochet, treble

ABBREVIATIONS
ch chain	ch sp chain space
htr half treble	ss slip stitch
nxt next	tch turning chain
RS right side	WS wrong side
rep repeat	tr treble

METHOD
Body (for both front and back)
Using the 2.00mm hook, make a chain of 135/143/151. This includes two extra chains for base row.
Work 1htr into fifth chain from hook, 1ch *miss 1ch, 1htr, 1ch rep* to last 2ch, 1htr into last ch of base row. 66/70/74 spaces.
Row 1 (WS): 2ch, work 1htr, 1ch into each 1ch sp until last 1ch sp, work 1htr into space, 1htr into second ch of tch, turn.
Row 2: 3ch, miss first 2htr, 1htr into nxt 1ch sp, *1ch, 1htr into each 1ch sp rep* to tch, 1ch 1htr into second ch of tch, turn.
Repeat the last two rows until work measures 39/40.5/42cm (15½/16/16½in).
End with a WS row.

Front top shaping
With RS facing, work 3ch, miss first 2htr *1htr, 1ch into nxt space*, 31/33/35 times, turn.
Nxt, miss first ch sp, work 1htr, 1ch 25/27/29 times, turn, miss first ch sp, work 1htr, 1ch 23/25/27 times, turn.
Miss first ch sp, work 1htr, 1ch 21/23/35 times, turn.
*Miss first ch sp, work 1htr, 1ch 19/21/23 times, turn.
Miss first ch sp, work 1htr, 1ch 17/19/21 times, turn*.
Continue to work as set, working 1htr, 1ch, decreasing the number of times the repeats are worked by two on each row until all sizes have worked the row: miss first ch sp, work 1htr, 1ch 5 times.
Total of 12/13/14 rows worked.

Working on these remaining sts, work as main patt, rep until it measures 23/24/25cm (9/9½/10in) from end of top shaping (this forms the strap).
Turn work around and working with WS facing repeat the shaping for the other side.

Back top shaping
Work same as front shaping, but end after second row of strap.

To Make Up
Join side seams, starting 5cm (2in) from bottom edge.
Join straps by placing both front and back straps (with both RS facing outwards), join together with a flat seam.

Flowers (make five of each different colour)
Using a 2mm hook, make 8ch and join with a ss to form a ring.
Round 1: Work 2ch, 1htr into ring 14 times, join with a ss in first 2ch.
Round 2: Work 6ch, *miss 2htr, ss into nxt htr, 6ch, rep* to end, ss into first ch of row. Five loops made.
Round 3: Into first loop on ring, work 1dc, 2htr, 2tr, 2htr, 1dc, work the same into each loop, ss into first dc. Fasten off.

Finishing
Sew the flowers on to the top using the ends of each one. Place one flower of any colour over the back join of the strap, then place the rest of the flowers however you wish. Embroider the stems connecting the flowers using a running stitch.

Stripy dog blanket

This is the height of luxury for your favourite pooch. The blanket is striped in a durable half treble stitch, so it's tough and the multi-coloured stripes hide the dirt or hairs. The colours blend so it suits any shade of dog fur, but play around with the colours to get the perfect combination. Crochet the size of the blanket to the size of your dog. You can also use any yarn, so if you have lots of scraps and ends, it's a great way to use them all up. You may end up loving it so much that you keep the blanket for yourself!

MEASUREMENTS
Small: 95 x 75cm (37½ x 29½in)
Large: 134 x 107cm (53in x 107in)

MATERIALS
Rooster Almerino Aran (50g balls)
shade 301, Cornish; shade 302, Sugared Almond; shade 303, Strawberry Cream; shade 304, Mushroom; shade 305, Custard; shade 306, Gooseberry; shade 307, Brighton Rock; shade 308, Spiced Plum; shade 309, Ocean; shade 310, Rooster
x 1 ball of each shade (small size)
x 2 balls of each shade (large size)

Crochet hook: size 5.00mm

STITCHES USED
half treble

ABBREVIATIONS
ch chain   htr half treble
st stitch

METHOD
Change yarn colour on each row.

Make 114 (166)ch, turn.

Each row: 2ch (counts as first htr) work 1htr into each st to end, turn. Repeat.

Continue until work measures 75cm (29.5in) (small), 107cm (42in) (large). Fasten off.

To Make Up
Sew in yarn ends.

Striped hairbands

These hairbands are refreshingly quick, inexpensive and easy to make. They make ideal gifts and can be crocheted in a single evening. They're also an excellent beginner's project as well as good for learning how to join colours.

MATERIALS
Rowan Handknit Cotton (50g balls)
Yarn A: shade 219, Gooseberry x 1 ball
Yarn B: shade 253, Tope x 1 ball
Yarn C: shade 315, Double Choc x 1 ball
Yarn D: shade 254, Flame x 1 ball

Crochet hook: size 3.75mm

STITCHES USED
chain stitch, double crochet, slip stitch

ABBREVIATIONS
ch chain stitch   dc double crochet
ss slip stitch   st stitch

METHOD
Row 1: Using yarn A make 75ch, turn work.
Row 2: Make 1ch, miss first st of previous row, 1dc into each stitch along row, turn work.
Row 3: Change to yarn B. Make 1ch, miss first st of previous row, 1dc into each stitch along row, turn work. Break yarn.
Row 4: Change to yarn C, make 1ch, miss first st off previous row, 1dc into each stitch along row, fasten off last stitch. Fasten off.
Row 5: Using yarn D, make 25ch, join yarn onto last st of previous row. 1dc into each st along row, make 25ch. Fasten off (this row forms the ties).
Row 6: Using colour C join yarn back to last dc of previous row, 1dc into each dc st of previous row, turn work. Break yarn.
Row 7: Using colour B, make 1ch, miss first st of previous row, 1dc into each stitch along row, turn work. Break yarn.
Row 8: Using colour A, make 1ch, miss first st, 1dc into each stitch along row, turn work.
Row 9: 1 ss into each st along row, fasten off.

To Make Up
Sew in yarn ends.

Mesh bag

This bag is stylish enough to carry around even if it's empty. It is made up of two side pieces, a base and strap in Debbie Bliss cotton and the front and back panels in Colinette Point Five Yarn. The handle is made of rope covered in Debbie Bliss Cotton. Buttons are used to decorate the front and back mesh panels. The bag is great for all seasons; it can either be used as a beach bag or as a winter accessory.

MATERIALS
(50g balls)
Yarn A: Debbie Bliss Cotton DK, shade 15, Red x 4 balls
(100g hanks)
Yarn B: Colinette Point Five, shade Jamboree x 2 hanks
150cm (59in) rope/washing line
28 black shiny shirt buttons, 1cm (½in) diameter

Crochet hooks: size 3.00mm and size 5.00mm

STITCHES USED
double crochet, treble, chain, slip stitch

ABBREVIATIONS

ch chain	dc double crochet
ch sp chain space	tr treble
sp space	ss slip stitch
rem remaining	t-ch turning chain
rep repeat	st(s) stitch(es)
alt alternately	

METHOD
Bag base
Use yarn A and crochet hook size 3.00mm
Make 52ch.
Row 1: 1dc into second ch from hook, 1dc into each rem ch, 1t-ch.
Row 2: Miss first dc, 1dc into each rem dc, 1t-ch.
Rows 3–17: Rep Row 2 15 times.
Row 18: Miss first dc, 1dc into each rem dc to end of row, one extra dc into last dc. Turn to short side of piece and 1dc into each row, one extra dc into end row, turn to long side (base of piece), 1dc into base of each dc, one extra dc into end dc, 1dc into each row, one extra dc into end row. Fasten off.

Side panels
Use yarn A, crochet hook 3.00mm.
Make 20ch.
Row 1: 1dc into third ch from hook, 1dc into each rem ch, 3t-ch.
Row 2: Miss first dc, 2tr into next 2dc, (2ch, miss 2dc, 3tr into next 3dc) to end of row, 3t-ch.
Rows 3–18: Rep Row 2 16 times.
Row 19: Miss 2dc, 1tr. (2ch, miss 2dc, 3tr into next 3dc) twice. 2ch, miss 2ch, 1tr, miss 1tr, 3t-ch.
Row 20: 2ch, (miss 2ch and 1tr), 3tr into next 3sts, 2ch, miss 2ch, 3tr into next 3sts, 2ch, (miss 2ch and 1tr), 1tr, 3t-ch.
Row 21: Miss 2ch, 3tr into next 3sts, 2ch, miss 2ch, 4tr into next 4sts, 3t-ch.
Row 22: Miss first tr, 3tr into next 3sts, 2ch, miss 2ch, 4tr into next 4sts, 3t-ch.
Rows 23–29: Rep Row 22 seven times.
Row 30: Miss first st, 1dc into each st to end. Fasten off.

Front and back panels
Use yarn B and crochet hook 5.00 mm. Make 37ch.
Row 1: 1dc into third ch from hook, 1dc into each rem ch to end, 3t-ch.
Row 2: Miss first dc, (3tr into next 3dc, 2ch, miss 2dc) five times, 2ch, miss 2dc, 4tr into next 4dc, 3t-ch.
Rows 3–4: Rep Row 2 twice.
Row 5: Miss first tr, 3tr into next 3sts, 1dc, (ch7, miss 4sts, 1dc into fifth st) five times. Miss 1ch, 4tr into next 4sts, 3t-ch.
Row 6: Miss first tr, 1tr, 1dc, (6ch, 1dc into top of loop) five times. ch6, (miss 3ch and 1tr) 1dc into second tr, 2tr into next 2sts, 3t-ch.
Row 7: Miss 2sts, 4tr into next 4sts, 1dc. (7ch, 1dc into top of loop) four times. 7ch, 1dc into top of loop, 4tr into next 4sts, 3t-ch.

Row 8: Rep Row 6.

Row 9: Miss first tr, 2tr into next 2tr, miss 2ch, 1dc, (7ch, 1dc into top of loop) four times. 7ch, 1dc into fourth ch, miss 2ch, 2tr into next 2sts, 3t-ch.

Row 10: Rep Row 6.

Row 11: Rep Row 9.

Rows 12–17: Rep Rows 6 and 9 alt.

Row 18: Miss first tr, 1tr, 3ch, miss 3ch, (4ch, 1dc into top of loop) four times. 4ch, miss 3ch, 1tr into first tr, 2tr into next 2tr, 1t-ch.

Row 19: Miss first tr (2dc into next 2sts, miss 1st), repeat to end. Fasten off.

Using yarn B put hook through first chain space (1-ch sp) made on Round 1, yrh and pull yarn through, work 3ch. (1tr, 1ch, 2tr) all in the same 1-ch space (1ch, 2tr) twice in each of next three 1-ch sps. 1ch, 1ss in third of first 3ch. Fasten off.

To Make Up

Use yarn A, crochet hook 3.00mm.

Pin base to front panel. Join with 1 line dc. Rep with back panel.

Pin side panel to base, join with 1 line dc. Rep with other side panel.

Pin side panels to front, join with 1 line dc. Rep all around the bag joining all the side seams.

Weave in all ends, turn inside out.

Sew buttons on to intersections in the front and back mesh randomly, 14 on each side.

Handle

Use yarn A and crochet hook 3.00mm.

Make 8ch.

Row 1: 1dc into third ch from hook, 1dc into each rem ch to end, 1t-ch. (6sts).

Row 2: Miss first dc, 1dc into each rem ch to end, 1t-ch.

Rep Row 2 138 times, fasten off.

Double up the 150cm (59in) rope/washing line, securing with tape at both ends.

Enclose rope in the crochet strip, leaving four rows free. Join crochet with 1 line dc, enclosing rope as you join.

Sew flat ends into bag.

Weave in all yarn ends.

Tie bolero

This fashionable cardigan can either be tied at the front or wrapped and tied at either the side or the back. It is made using the very soft Debbie Bliss Baby Cashmerino in a delicate but simple stitch. It is an excellent garment either for the daytime, or when you want to dress up for the evening.

MEASUREMENTS

To fit bust sizes 76/86/97cm (30/34/38in)
Chest: 81/92/104cm (32/36/41in)
Length: 42/44/46cm (16½/17½/18in)
Sleeve length: 31/33/34cm (12¼/13/13½in)

MATERIALS

Debbie Bliss Baby Cashmerino (50g balls)
shade 609, Mauve x 8/9/10 balls

Crochet hooks: size 2.50mm, size 3.25mm and size 3.50mm

TENSION

26 stitches and 15 rows to 10cm (4in) over pattern on size 3.50mm crochet hook.

STITCHES USED

double crochet, slip stitch, treble

ABBREVIATIONS

ch chain	rep repeat
tr treble	dc double crochet
dec decrease	ss slip stitch
inc increase	nxt next
alt alternate	patt pattern
RS right side	WS wrong side
foll following	tch turning chain

METHOD

12st repeat plus 1st.
Row 1: (RS) 2tr into third ch from hook, * miss 2 ch, 1 dc into nxt ch, 5ch miss 5ch, 1dc into nxt ch, miss 2ch, 5tr into nxt ch, rep from * ending last rep with only 3tr into last ch, turn.
Row 2: 1ch, 1dc into first st, *5ch, 1dc into nxt 5ch arch, 5ch, 1dc into third tr of nxt 5tr; rep from * ending last rep with 1dc into top of tch. Turn.
Row 3: *5ch, 1dc into nxt 5 arch, 5tr into nxt dc, 1dc into nxt arch, rep from * ending 2ch, 1tr into last dc, miss tch, turn.
Row 4: 1ch, 1dc into first st, *5ch, 1dc into third tr of nxt 5tr, 5ch, 1dc into nxt 5ch arch, rep from * to end, turn.
Row 5: 3ch (count as 1tr), 2tr into first st, * 1dc into nxt arch, 5ch 1dc into nxt arch, 5tr into nxt dc; rep from * ending last rep with only 3tr into last dc, miss tch, turn.
Repeat Rows 2, 3, 4 and 5.

Back

Using 3.50mm hook, make 111/123/135 chain (includes 2ch extra for base row).
Commence pattern by repeating the first row of the 12st pattern across base chain, turn. Do 9/10/11 repeats.
Continue working patt as set, repeating Rows 2, 3, 4 and 5.
Work till patt measures 22/22.5/24cm (8⅝/8⅞/9½in), ending with RS facing for nxt row.
Shape armhole (when shaping count every ch, dc, tr as 1st).
Ss across first 3sts, 1dc into nxt st, patt to last 4sts, 1dc into nxt st, turn.
Nxt row: Rep last row once more, turn.
Now work patt as set till armhole measures 18/18/20cm (7/7/8in). End with RS facing for nxt row.

Back neck shaping

Work three repeats of patt for size 1 and 2. Size 3 work 3.5 repeats. (37/37/43sts.) This includes first st.
Nxt row: Ss across first 6sts, patt to end, turn.
Nxt row: Patt to end.
Nxt row: Ss across 6sts, patt to end. Fasten off. (25/25/31 sts.)
With RS facing, miss nxt four arches. Join yarn to nxt dc, foll patt to end.
Now work neck as above but reverse shaping. Fasten off.

Left front

As before when decreasing, count every ch, dc, and tr as 1st each. Using 3.50mm hook, make 147/153/159 ch.
Now follow pattern repeat as set for back.12/12.5/13 patt repeats.

First and third sizes

Work two rows. RS facing for nxt row.

Second size

Row 1: Work to last rep then miss 2ch, 1dc into nxt ch, 2ch, miss 2ch, 1tr into last st, turn.
Nxt Row: Work as Row 4.

All sizes

Now continue with patt as set. Work the following shaping:
With RS facing for nxt row.
Work to last 18sts then 3tr (3tr; 2ch 1tr) into nxt dc, turn.
Nxt row: Ss across first 18sts patt to end, turn.
Nxt row: Patt to last 18sts then work 2ch 1tr into nxt dc (5ch, 1dc into nxt arch; 2ch, 1tr into nxt dc), turn.
Nxt row: This row and 5/5/4 alternate rows, dec 6sts at inner edge, ending with WS facing for nxt row.
Nxt row: Work to end. 55/61/67sts remain.
Nxt row: This row and foll 7/9/10 alt rows, dec 3sts at inner edge, ending with WS. At same time, when having worked the same number of rows as back to armhole, start armhole shaping as follows:
RS facing.
Ss across first 3sts, 1dc into nxt st, patt as set.
Nxt row: Patt to last 4sts, dc into nxt st, turn.
When having worked all the decreases, 25/25/31sts remain. Continue straight until armhole measures same as back to end of back neck shaping. Fasten off.

Right front

Work same as left front reversing all shaping.

Sleeves (both alike)
First size only

Using size 2.50mm hook, make 63ch.

Work patt as set for back, work six rows, ending with RS facing for nxt row. Change to size 3.50mm hook.

Second and third sizes

Using size 3.50mm hook throughout, make 63/75ch.
Work six rows as set by back, ending with RS facing for nxt row.
5/5/6 patt repeats.
Now start side shaping:
Row 7 (inc row): 8ch, 1dc into first arch, *5tr into nxt dc, 1dc into nxt arch, 5ch, 1dc into nxt five arches, rep from *to last two arches then work 5tr into nxt dc, 1dc into nxt arch, 5ch, 1tr into last dc, turn.
Row 8: 1ch, 1dc into first st, 3ch, 1dc into 5ch arch, patt as Row 4 of main patt to last arch, 3ch, 1dc into same loop, turn.
Row 9: 1ch, 1dc into first st, * 5tr into nxt dc, 1dc into nxt 5ch arch, 5ch, 1dc into nxt 5ch arch, rep from * to last arch, 5tr into nxt dc, 1dc into last dc, turn.
Row 10: 1ch, 1dc into first st, 3ch, 1dc into third tr of nxt 5tr, * 5ch, 1dc into nxt 5ch arch, 5ch, 1dc into third tr of nxt 5tr, rep from * to last 5tr group, 5ch, 1dc into third tr of nxt 5tr, 2ch, 1tr into last st, turn.
Row 11 (inc row): 3ch, 2tr into first st, 1dc into 2ch arch, then patt as Row 5 of main patt to end, working 5ch, 1dc into last 3ch arch, 3tr into last st, turn.
Rows 12–14 inclusive: Work as main patt Rows 2–4.
Row 15 (inc row): Work as Row 5 of main patt but work 4tr instead of 2tr at beg of row and 5tr instead of 3tr at end of row.
Row 16: As Row 10 (above).
Row 17: Work as Row 5 of main patt, omitting first 3ch, 2tr and last 3tr, work 1ch, 1dc into first st, 5ch, 1dc into 5ch arch, work to end with 1dc into last st, turn.
Row 18: As Row 2 of main patt to last arch, work 3ch, 1dc into last st, turn.
Row 19 (inc row): Work as Row 3 of main patt but work 5ch, 1dc into first 3ch arch, work to end.
Rows 20–22 inclusive: Work Rows 4/5/2 of main patt , then rep Rows 7–19 inclusive 9/9/10 patt repeats remain.

Now work 11/13/15 rows straight, ending with RS facing for nxt row.

Shape armhole

Ss across 3sts, 1dc into nxt st, work to last 4sts, 1dc into nxt st, turn.

Nxt row: Repeat last row once more. Fasten off.

To Make Up

Press all pieces lightly. Sew shoulder, side and sleeve seams using a flat seam stitch.

Edgings

Body

With RS facing, starting at lower left side seam, and using 3.00mm hook, work as follows:

Row 1: Work 1dc into foundation row, * 4ch, 1dc* (1 arch made) evenly spaced, rep from * to * along all edges, taking care not to let the arches be too deep, ss into first dc, do not turn.

Row 2: Work 4dc into each arch end, ss into first dc, fasten off.

Lower sleeve edging

Work the same as for body.

Fasten off.

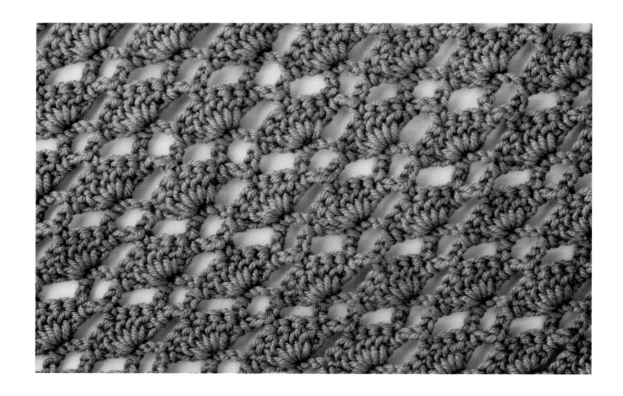

Flower-power beaded belt

This beaded belt is full of character, bright and colourful with pretty beads and an attractive bow that ties at the front or the side. Wear it with jeans or over a skirt. The flowers are a feature that make the belt a perfect accessory for any garment.

SIZES
Small: 8–12 flowers
Medium: 12–16 flowers
Large: 16–18 flowers

MATERIALS
Debbie Bliss Cotton DK (50g balls)
Choose 3 balls from the following colours:
shade 37, Lilac
shade 36, Orange
shade 35, Yellow
shade 38, Pink
shade 15, Red
shade 20, Light Green
shade 31, Purple

Crochet hook: size 4.50mm

Approx: 2.4m (94½in) ribbon, 15mm (⅝in) wide
22 assorted beads big enough for yarn to thread through
2 beads with big enough hole for ribbon to go through

STITCHES USED
slip stitch, treble, treble two together

ABBREVIATIONS
ch chain
ss slip stitch
dc double crochet
tr treble
tr2tog treble two together as follows over next 2dc:
Yrh, insert hook into next st, yrh and pull through. Yrh, pull through two loops (leaving two loops on hook). Yrh, insert hook into next st and pull through. Yrh, pull through two loops, yrh and pull through all three loops.

METHOD
Leaving a long tail (approx 15.5cm [6in]), make 6ch, join with ss to make a ring.

Round 1: Work 18dc into ring catching tail into chain, ss into first dc.

Round 2: *3ch tr2tog (see abbreviations), 3ch, ss into next dc*. Repeat * to * five more times. (Six petals). Place last ss into last dc of previous round. Fasten off.

Pull tail from first 6ch to tighten flower hole.

To Make Up
Attaching beads and flowers
1. Thread needle with same colour yarn as one of the flowers.
2. Insert needle into same colour flower with a secure stitch.
3. Thread one bead through needle and onto yarn. Push bead up close to flower, make a secure stitch into second flower and thread yarn back through bead to first flower, make a secure stitch and fasten off.
4. Weave in ends.

Attaching the ribbon
Cut ribbon to two lengths of 1.2m (47in) long.
1. With one piece of ribbon and belt wrong side facing, thread end of ribbon up through the gap (between the 3ch and the tr2tog) of petal opposite beads and back downwards through the gap on the adjacent petal.
2. Turn belt to right side facing. Pull ribbon through so you have two equal lengths.
3. Thread both ends of ribbon through a needle with a large eye. It's easier to fold the ribbon in half before threading through. Push needle through bead and push bead up towards flower. Trim ends of ribbon to fit so it sits close to flower just touching the edges.

Repeat on other end.

Summer brimmed hat

This is a cool and stylish way to keep the sun's rays off your face, especially when styled with your aviator sunglasses. A must-have for every conscientious girl who wants to keep the sun off; it scrunches up, easily fits into a bag and creates an ultra cool look.

MEASUREMENTS
One size: 50cm (20in)

MATERIALS
(50g balls)
Rowan Handknit Cotton
Yarn A: shade 219, Gooseberry x 1 ball
Yarn B: shade 318, Seafarer x 1 ball
Rowan Cotton Glacé
Yarn C: shade 815, Excite x 1 ball
Yarn D: shade 812, Ivy x 1 ball

Crochet hooks: size 2.00 mm and size 4.00mm

STITCHES USED
chain, double crochet, double treble, half treble, treble, triple treble, slip stitch

ABBREVIATIONS

ch chain	dc double crochet
sp space	ss slip stitch
tr treble	WS wrong side
RS right side	trtr triple treble
htr half treble	rep repeat
dtr double treble	

TENSION
6ch x 5 rows to 5cm (2in) using size 4.50mm hook using half treble.

METHOD
Using 4.50mm hook and yarn A make 5ch. Join with ss to make a ring.

Round 1: Make 3 ch. Work *1htr into circle, 1ch*. Repeat *to* six more times. Join with ss to second of 3ch.

Round 2: Make 3ch. *1htr 1ch 1htr 1ch in each sp between htrs. Repeat from * to end. Join with ss to second of 3ch.

Round 3: Using yarn B make 3ch. 1htr, 1ch in same ch sp *1htr 1ch 1htr 1ch into next ch sp. 1htr 1ch into next ch sp*. Repeat from *to* to end. Join with ss to second of 3ch.

Round 4: Make 3ch. Miss first sp. *Work 1htr, 1ch into next sp*. Repeat from *to* to end. Join with ss to second of 3ch.

Round 5: Using yarn A make 3ch. 1htr in first sp, 1ch. *1htr 1ch twice in next sp. 1htr 1ch into each of next 2sps*. Repeat from *to* to last sp. 1htr 1ch. Join with ss as before.

Round 6: As Round 4.

Round 7: Using yarn B make 3ch. Work 1htr 1ch in first sp*. 1htr 1ch in next 2sps. 1htr 1ch 1htr 1ch in next sp*. Repeat from *to* to end. Join with ss in second of 3ch.

Rounds 8–12: As Round 4, but change yarns on Round 9 to yarn A and on Round 11 to yarn B

Rounds 13–16: As Round 4, but change yarns on Round 13 to yarn A and on Round 15 to yarn B.

Round 17: Same as Round 4, using yarn A.

Rounds 18 to 21: As Rounds 4 and 6 but change yarns on Round 19 to B and Round 21 to A.

Round 22: As Round 12.

Brim

Round 1: Using yarn B make 3ch, *2htr in next sp six times, 1htr in next sp*. Rep from * to * until end. Join with ss to second of 3ch.

Round 2: Make 3ch, *1htr in sp between htrs four times, 2htr in next sp*. Rep from * to * until end. Join with ss to second of 3ch.

Round 3: Change to yarn A and work as in Round 2.

Round 4: Make 3ch. * 1htr in each sp.* Rep from * to * until end. Join with ss to second of 3ch.

Round 5: Change to yarn B. Make 3ch. * 1htr in next sp nine times, 2htrs in next sp.* Rep from * to * until end. Join with ss to second of 3ch.

Rounds 6–9: As Round 5 but change yarn on Round 7 to yarn A and Round 9 to yarn B.

Round 10: Using two ends of yarn C make 2ch. 1dc in each sp to end. Join with ss and fasten off.

Flowers

In yarn C, using only one end make 49ch.

Row 1: 1dc in fourth ch from hook, *2ch, miss 2ch, 1dc in next ch.* Rep to end. 1ch, turn.

Row 2: 3dc in sp four times, 4tr in next sp three times, 5tr in next sp twice, 4dtr in next sp, 5dtr in next sp twice, 4trtr in next sp, 5trtr in next sp twice, 3trtr in last sp.

With RS facing, and starting at the beginning of Row 2, roll up the work and sew together through the foundation chain to form a rose. To make a more open flower sew it together with WS facing.

Leaf

In yarn D make 11ch. 1dc in second ch from hook, 1dc, 1htr, 3tr, 1htr, 2dc, 3dc in last ch. Continue working down the other side of the foundation ch until the end. Join with a ss. Fasten off.

To Make Up

Using yarn C sew the flower on to the hat where you would like it to be placed. Using yarn D sew the leaves on to make a little posy. Neatly sew in all the yarn ends.

Patterns... to get you hooked

Daisy cashmere scarf

Making crochet squares is the perfect occupation for snatched moments, as you only make one square at a time. This crochet-square scarf is made out of Debbie Bliss Baby Cashmerino using simple crochet stitches and is beautifully soft.

MATERIALS
Debbie Bliss Baby Cashmerino (50g balls)
Yarn A (main colour): shade 609, Purple x 2 balls
Yarn B: shade 600, Pink x 1 ball
Yarn C: shade 503, Green x 1 ball
Yarn D: shade 203, Teal x 1 ball

Crochet hook: size 3.25mm
The scarf is made up of 34 squares joined together, edged with a double crochet stitch and decorated with mini pom-poms.

STITCHES USED
double crochet, treble, three-treble cluster, half treble, slip stitch

ABBREVIATIONS
ch chain
ch sp chain space
tr treble
sp space
RS right side

dc double crochet
htr half treble
yrh yarn round hook
ss slip stitch

How to make a three-treble cluster

1. Wrap the yarn round the hook (yrh), insert hook into stitch, yrh and draw through to the front, yrh and draw through two loops (two loops remain on the hook).
2. Yrh, insert hook into the stitch, yrh and draw through to the front, yrh and draw through two loops (three loops remain on the hook).
3. Repeat step 2. There will be four loops remaining on the hook.
4. Yrh and pull through all four loops. This completes your three-treble cluster.

METHOD

Using yarn A make 6ch. Join with a ss in first ch to form a ring.

Round 1 (RS): Using yarn A make 3ch (this counts as one treble). Make 1tr into the ring, *1ch, 2tr in ring*. Repeat from * to * twice more. Make 1ch, 1ss in top of first 3ch. Fasten off.

Round 2: Using yarn B slip stitch into first chain space (ch sp), made on Round 1, make 3ch. 1tr, 1ch, 2tr all in the same ch space. 1ch, 2tr twice in each of next 3ch sps. 1ch, 1ss in top of first 3ch. Fasten off.

Round 3: Using yarn C join with ss in first ch sp made on Round 2. 3ch, work 1tr, 1ch, 2tr all in the same ch sp. 1ch, 2tr twice in each of next 7ch sps, 1ch, 1ss in top of first 3ch. Fasten off.

Round 4: Using yarn D. Join with a ss in second ch sp made on Round 3. 3ch, make 1 cluster, make 4 ch, make 1 cluster into same ch sp. *3ch, make 1htr into second ch sp along, 3ch, make 1 cluster, 4ch, 1 cluster into second ch sp along*. Repeat *to* twice more, until you have four corners. 3ch, make 1htr into second ch sp along, 3ch, ss into top st of first 3ch. Don't fasten off.

Round 5: Continue using yarn D. 1ch, *1dc in top of next 2sts. 4dc in next ch sp. 1dc into top of next 2sts. 3dc in next ch sp. 1dc in top of htr. 3dc in next ch sp.* Repeat from * to * three more times. Ss into top of next st. Fasten off. Use different colour combinations for each square. Make 34 squares.

To Make up

Place squares together in a line, two squares wide. With RS facing and using yarn A, join squares with a double crochet into each stitch, up centre line (vertically), then join squares across (horizontally) so that all squares are joined together.

Edging

Use yarn A.

With RS facing, join yarn with ss.

Make a double crochet into every stitch across top, sides and bottom of scarf until you have finished one row.

Cast off.

Neatly sew in ends.

Add some mini pom-poms (see page 129).

Attaching mini pom-poms to scarf

1. Take a piece of yarn the same colour as pom-pom and join to edge of scarf.
2. Make 4ch.
3. Pick up a mini pom-pom and push hook into two of the loops that are holding the pom-pom together in its centre.
4. Slip stitch to pull yarn through and cast off.
5. Break yarn and cut to blend in with pom-pom.
6. Sew yarn ends in neatly.
7. Fluff up pom-pom with a brush. Hold pom-pom very firmly and softly brush with quick sharp motion.

Attach five pom-poms to each end of the scarf.

Fingerless gloves

These fingerless gloves, a mixture of Debbie Bliss Alpaca and Silk, are the height of luxury and indulgence. They are very simple to make and elegant and comfortable to wear. Crocheted in the round, the ruffle and the thumbhole are the last parts to be made. The thumbhole is formed by Rounds 22–23.

MATERIALS
Debbie Bliss Alpaca Silk DK (50g balls)
shade 12, Green x 2 balls

Crochet hook: size 3.75mm

STITCHES USED
chain stitch, double crochet, slip stitch, treble, double treble

ABBREVIATIONS

ch chain stitch	st stitch
sts stitches	dc double crochet
tr treble	dtr double treble
ss slip stitch	

METHOD
Make 36ch, join into a round using a ss.

Round 1: 1ch, miss first st, 1dc in each remaining st in round, ending with a ss into the first dc.
Round 2: 6ch, miss 3sts, 1tr, * 3ch, miss 3sts, 1tr. Repeat from * seven times. 3ch, ss into third of first 6ch in round.
Round 3: 1ch, miss first st, 1dc into each remaining st in round, finish round with a ss into the first dc.
Rounds 4–9: As Round 3.
Round 10: 1ch, miss first st, 4dc, * miss next st, 4dc, Repeat from * to end of round, ending with a ss.
Round 11: 1ch, miss first st, 1dc into each remaining st in round, ending with a ss.
Round 12: 1ch, miss first st, * 3 dc, 2dc into next st. Repeat from * to end of round, ending with a ss.
Rounds 13–21: As Round 3.

Round 22: Left glove: 1ch, miss first st, 2dc, 5ch, miss 5 sts, 1dc into next st, 1dc into each remaining st in round, ending with 1ss. (For right glove: 1ch, miss first st, 1dc into each st until last 7sts, 5ch, miss 5sts, 1dc into next st, 1dc into next st, ss.)
Round 23: 1ch, miss first st, 1dc into each st in round (including 5ch sts of previous round). Ending with a ss.
Rounds 24–26: As Round 3.
Round 27: 1ch, miss first st, 8dc, miss next st, 8dc, miss next st, 8dc, miss next st, 1dc into each remaining st, ending with a ss.
Rounds 28–30: As Round 3.
Round 31: *5ch, miss 3 sts, 1dc into next st. Repeat from * to end.
Round 32: *5ch, 1dc into third ch of first 5ch loop. Repeat from * to end.
Round 33: As Round 32, fasten off last st.

Thumb
Rejoin yarn to thumbhole created by Rounds 22–23.
Round 1: 1dc into each of 5sts at top of hole and follow round to 1dc in each of 5sts at bottom of thumbhole, join to first st with 1ss.
Round 2: 1ch, miss first st, 1dc into each st, join with a ss.
Rounds 3–5: As Round 2.
Fasten off.

Ruffle
Join yarn onto first tr st, at wrist end of glove.
*Make 7dtr along this st (around the stitch itself, not into it).
1dtr into second of 3sts at base of st.
Make 7dtr along next tr st (around the stitch itself, not into it).
1dtr into second of 3sts at top of st.* Repeat until the ruffle meets up around wrist. Join together with 1ss.
Fasten off.

Beaded purse

Beaded crochet is at the height of fashion, seen accompanying the most high-profile of couture on the catwalks. This pretty purse has delicate pearl beads and a pull-string tie.

MATERIALS
Rooster Almerino Aran (50g balls)
Yarn A: shade 301, Cornish x 1 ball
Yarn B: shade 307, Brighton Rock x 1 ball
Approx 100 Pearl White Mill Hill Glass pebble beads

Crochet hook size: 3.00mm

STITCHES USED
double crochet, slip stitch, treble, double treble

ABBREVIATIONS
ch chain	inc increase
ss slip stitch	dc double crochet
dtr double treble	tr treble

METHOD
All stitches are worked into the back of the stitch to create a ridge.

Using yarn A make 4ch. Join with a ss in first ch to form a ring. (After each round, join with a ss).

Round 1: Work 8dc into ring.
Round 2: (1dc, inc in next st) four times (12sts).
Round 3: (1dc, inc in next st) six times (18sts).
Round 4: (1dc, inc in next st) nine times (27sts).
Round 5: (2dc, inc in next st) nine times (36sts).
Round 6: 1dc into each st (36sts).
Round 7: (3dc, inc in next st) nine times (45sts).
Round 8: 1dc into each st (45sts).
Round 9: (4dc, inc in next st) nine times (54sts).
Round 10: 1dc into each st (54sts).
Round 11: (5dc, inc in next st) nine times (63sts).

Round 12: 1dc into each st (63sts).
Round 13: Dtr into each st (63sts).
Round 14: *1ch, insert bead, 1dc into every other st* (63sts).
Round 15: 1tr into each st (63sts).
Round 16: 1dc into each st (63sts).
Round 17: *dtr into each st, insert bead every other dtr* (63sts).
Round 18: 1dc into each st (63sts).
Round 19: *1ch, dtr into every other st* (63sts).
Round 20: 1dc into every st (63sts).
Round 21: 1tr into every st (63sts).
Round 22: *1dc into every st, insert bead every other dc* (63sts).
Round 23: *1ch, dtr into every other st* (63sts).
Round 24: 1dc into every st (63sts).
Round 25: 1tr into every st (63sts).
Round 26: *1ch, 1tr into every other st* (63sts).
Round 27: Dtr into every st (63sts).
Round 28: *1ch, 1tr into every other st* (63sts).
Round 29: Dtr into every st (63sts).
Round 30: *1ch, 1tr into every other st * (62sts), Fasten off.

Handle
The handle is made by creating a long ribbon, which is threaded through Round 27 of the purse.
Using yarn B make a 200ch.
Insert hook into third chain from hook. Work 197tr into chain. Fasten off.

Picot edge
Using yarn B
1ss into first st, (5ch, ss into third ch from hook, 2ch, miss 2st, 1ss into next st) repeat to end, fasten off.

Ribbon slippers

Cosy, cute and very sought after, in recent trends crochet slippers have been a key feature of the high-street shops. Everyone will be envious of these beautiful handmade slippers with a pretty flower and ribbon.

MEASUREMENTS
Small size approximately UK size 1–3
Medium size approximately UK size 4–5
Large size approximately UK size 5–6

MATERIALS
(50g balls)
For slippers:
Debbie Bliss Cashmerino Chunky, shade 11 x 2 balls
2m (78in) of 10mm (⅛in) wide ribbon
For flower:
Oddments of yarn or x 1 ball each of Debbie Bliss Merino DK shade 700, Red and shade 703, Pink

Crochet hooks: size 4.50mm for slippers; size 3.25mm for flower motif

STITCHES USED
double crochet, half treble, slip stitch, treble, treble two together

ABBREVIATIONS

ch chain	dc double crochet
htr half treble	RS right side facing
ss slip stitch	sts stitches
tr treble	tr2tog treble two together (see panel above right)

dec decrease: *insert hook into next st, pull loop through, repeat from * once, yrh and pull through all three loops (this decreases 1 stitch).

Tip: Tr2tog: work 1tr into each of next 2dc. Yrh, insert hook into next dc, draw yarn through, yrh and draw through two loops on hook (two loops remain). Yrh, insert hook into next dc, draw yarn through, yrh and draw through two loops on hook (three loops remain). Yrh and draw through the three loops on hook. Yrh wrap yarn around hook.

METHOD
Soles
Make 20/24/28 ch (3 sizes).

Row 1: Work 2htr into second ch from hook, 2htr into next ch, 1htr into each of next 15/19/23ch, 2htr into next ch, 3htr into last chain. Working into other side of chain, work 2htr into next ch, 1htr in each of the next 15/19/23sts. 2htr in next st, 1htr into first ch sp at beginning of work. With ss join into top of first htr.

Row 2: Work 2ch (counts as 1htr), 1htr in same space, 2htr into each of the next 2sts, 1htr into each of next 4sts. 1dc in each of next 11/15/19sts, 1htr in each of next 2sts, 2htr in each of next 5sts, 1htr in each of next 2sts, 1dc in each of next 11/15/19sts, 1htr in each of next 4sts, 2 htr in each of next 2sts. Join with ss into top of second ch.

Row 3: Work 3ch, 1tr into same sp. 2tr in each of next 4sts, 1tr into next st, 1htr into next 7/9/11sts. 1dc in each of next 11/13/15sts, *2dc into next st, 1dc into next st, Repeat from * once. *1dc into next st, 2dc into next st. Repeat from * once. 1dc into each of the next 11/13/15sts, 1 htr into each of next 7/9/11sts. 1tr into next st, 2tr in each of the next 3sts. Join with a ss into top of 3ch.

Row 4: Work 2ch, 1htr in same space, 2htr in each of next 6sts. 1htr in each of next 4 sts, 1dc in each of next 21/25/29sts. 2dc in each of next 6sts, 1dc in each of next 21/25/29sts, 1htr in each of next 4sts, 2htr in each remaining sts. Join to first st and fasten off.

Make three more soles as above.

Upper slipper

With RS of sole facing, join yarn in any stitch at heel. Working in the back loop of stitches throughout.

Round 1: Put in a round marker and join yarn slightly to the right or left of centre. 1dc in each stitch of round. Join with ss.

Round 2: Take out round marker and place a different coloured marker at the centre of the toe and another at the centre of the heel. 1dc into each st, until 3sts from the centre of the toe. Dec 3sts (see Abbreviations). Continue 1dc into each st until 3sts from the centre marker of the heel.

Round 3: Dec 3sts. 1dc into each st until 4sts from the centre marker of the toe. Dec 2sts, 1dc, dec 2sts. 1dc into each st until marker of heel.

Round 4: 1dc into each st until approximately halfway down the side between the toe and heel (instep), dec 1st. Place a marker. Continue 1dc into each st until the toe marker. Dec 1st at centre of toe. Continue 1dc in each st until approximately in centre of heel and toe, opposite where marker for instep has been placed. Dec 1st. Take instep marker out. Continue 1dc in each st until heel marker.

Round 5: Work 1dc into to each st until 3sts from toe marker. Dec 3sts. Continue 1dc in each st until heel marker.

Round 6: Work 1dc into each st until 4sts from toe marker. Dec 2sts, 1dc, dec 2sts. Continue 1dc in each st until 1st before heel marker.

Round 7: Dec 1st at heel. Continue 1dc in each st until 4sts before centre of toe marker. Dec 2sts, 1dc, dec 2sts. Continue 1dc in each st until heel marker.

Round 8: 1dc into each st until 6sts before centre of toe marker. Dec 2sts *insert hook into next st, pull loop through, repeat three times from *, yrh, pull through all loops at one time, dec 2sts. 1dc in each remaining st until 2sts before heel marker, ss into the next 2sts to even the round.

Round 9: 3ch, miss 1st, 1htr in next st, *1ch, miss 1st, 1htr in next st, repeat from * until end of round. 1ch, join with ss into top of third chain. Fasten off.

Flower

Make 6ch, join with ss to form a ring.

Round 1: 1ch, work 15dc into ring, ss into first dc.

Round 2: *3ch tr2tog (see Abbreviations) over next 2dc. 3ch,

ss into next dc*. Repeat * to * four more times (five petals). Place last ss into last dc of previous round. Fasten off.

Round 3: Using yarn C, join with 1ss in any stitch of one of the petals. *1ch, work 1dc into top of next st *, rep from * to * until end.

Pull tail from first 6ch to tighten flower hole.

Sew in ends.

To Make Up

Stitch one sole onto bottom of each slipper, so that slipper is strengthened by having two soles.

Thread ribbon through loop holes and tie with a bow at the back.

Attach the flower at the front.

Hot-water bottle cover

Toasty warm, this hot-water bottle cover is made with superchunky Rowan Big Wool in soft, cosy colours. It's too good to put under the covers and needs to be shown off!

MEASUREMENTS
To fit an average sized hot-water bottle: 26cm (10¼in) width x 37cm (14½in) depth (includes top gathering).

MATERIALS
Rowan Big Wool (100g balls)
shade 029, Pistachio x 2 balls
shade 014, Whoosh x 2 balls
shade 001, White Hot x 1 ball

Crochet hook: size 5.50mm

TENSION
11dc stitches and 13 rows to 10cm (4in) on size 5.50mm crochet hook (or hook size to achieve correct tension).

STITCHES USED
double crochets, slip stitch

ABBREVIATIONS
ch chain
RS right side
foll following

dc double crochet
nxt next
ss slip stitch

METHOD
Front and back (both alike)
Using 5.50mm hook and yarn colour Whoosh (pink), make 29ch. Work 1dc into second ch from hook, then 1dc into each ch to end, turn. Do not fasten off.
Next row: Change to colour Pistachio (pale green), work 1ch,*1dc* into each dc to end. Turn, do not fasten off. Change to colour White Hot, work one row as last row. Keeping the repeat as set, carry each yarn not in use up the side of the work, work a total of 40 rows.

With RS facing work eyelet row, keeping colour repeat as set throughout, as follows:
1dc, * 1ch, miss 1ch, 1dc into nxt 2dc, rep from * to end, turn.
Next row: Work one row of dcs working 1dc into each 1ch space. Work a further four rows of dc.
Fasten off.

To Make Up
Sew both side seams using a flat seam stitch, leaving top open. With RS facing and using Whoosh, using size 5.50mm crochet hook, work picot edging as follows:
Starting at top side seam, ss into dc of previous row, 1ch, 1dc into nxt 2dc * make picot by working 3ch, ss into third ch from hook, miss 1dc, 1dc into nxt 3dc, rep from * to last 3dc, 1 picot, miss 1dc, 1dc into last st, ss into first dc, fasten off.

Using a length of each colour yarn, make a plait 145cm (57in) long, leaving a length of 10cm (4in) of each colour at each end of plait (use these three lengths to tie the pom-poms onto each end of the plait). Thread plait through the eyelets so that each end finishes in middle of front of cover.

Pom-poms (make 2)
Cut two circles of card measuring 5cm (2in). Mark out a smaller circle in the middle of each card, cut out.
Using the three colours separately, wrap yarn around the two cards together until it is tightly packed with yarn.
With a pair of narrow-ended scissors, cut between the two cards, slightly part the cards and using the loosed ends of each plait, tie into the centre of the pom-pom. Pull tightly and knot. Ease off both pieces of card and fluff up the pom-pom, trimming the outer edges to form a smooth ball. Repeat for the second pom-pom.

When the hot-water bottle is in its cover, pull the ties and make a bow to form a fit around the neck of the bottle.

Cushion cake

This cushion is made of two identical pieces of crochet attached together. It's quick and easy and helps you get to grips with working in rounds. The yarn is soft and luxurious and a complete pleasure to work with. The edging uses a fuchsia pink from the Debbie Bliss Cashmerino Aran range that gives it a touch of glamour and the little flower adds a splash of contrasting colour. It looks good enough to eat.

MEASUREMENTS

Makes cushion cover to fit a 40.6cm (16in) round cushion pad

MATERIALS

(50g balls)

Yarn A (main colour): Rooster Almerino Aran, shade 301, Cornish x 3 balls

Yarn B (edging): Debbie Bliss Cashmerino Aran, shade 616, Fuchsia x 1 ball

Yarn C (flower): Debbie Bliss Alpaca Silk DK, shade 012, Green x 1 ball (alternatively, use oddments)

Yarn D (flower): Rooster Almerino Aran, shade 307, Brighton Rock x 1 ball (alternatively, use oddments)

Crochet hooks: size 5.00mm, size 3.25mm

STITCHES USED

double crochet, half treble, slip stitch, treble, treble two together

ABBREVIATIONS

ch chain	ch chain space
dc double crochet	htr half treble
MC main colour	rem remaining
RS right side facing	ss slip stitch
tr2tog treble two together	tr treble

Tip: Tr2tog as follows over next 2dc: Yrh, insert hook into next st, yrh and pull through. Yrh, pull through two loops (leaving two loops on hook). Yrh insert hook into next st and pull through. Yrh, pull through two loops, yrh and pull through all three loops.

METHOD

The number of rounds you need to make to cover your cushion will depend on your tension. You may need to make one round less. Measure your work against your cushion pad when nearing the end.

Front and back (both alike)

Don't turn at end of rounds, work with RS facing.
Use MC (yarn A) and hook size 5.00mm make 4ch and join with a ss in first ch to form a ring.

Round 1 (RS): 3ch (these 3ch at the beginning of rounds count as the first tr), make 11tr in ring, 1ss in third of first 3tr.

Round 2: 3ch, 1tr in same st as ss, 2tr in each of rem tr, 1ss in third of first 3ch. (24sts)

Round 3: 3ch, 1tr in same place as ss, *1tr in next tr, 2tr in each of next 2tr; rep from *to last 2tr, 1tr in next tr, 2tr in last tr, 1ss in third of first 3ch. (40sts)

Round 4: 3ch, 1tr in same place as ss, *1tr in each of next 3tr, 2tr in next tr; rep from * to last 3tr, 1tr in each of last 3tr, 1ss in third of first 3ch. (50sts)

Round 5: 3ch, 1tr in same place as ss. *1tr in each of next 4tr, 2tr in next tr; rep from * to last 4tr, 1tr in each of last 4tr, 1ss in third of first 3ch. (60sts)

Round 6: 3ch, 1tr in same place as ss, *1tr in each of next 5tr, 2tr in next tr; rep from * to last 5tr, 1tr in each of last 5tr, 1ss in third of first 3ch. (70sts)

Round 7: 3ch, 1tr in same place as ss, * 1tr in each of next 6tr, 2tr in next tr; rep from * to last 6tr; 1tr in each of last 6tr, 1ss in third of first 3ch. (80sts)

Round 8: 3ch, 1tr in same place as ss, *1tr in each of next 7tr, 2tr in next tr; rep from * to last 7tr, 1tr in each of last 7tr, 1ss in third of first 3ch. (90sts)

Round 9: 3ch, 1tr in same place as ss, *1tr in each of next 8tr, 2tr in next tr. Rep from *to last 8tr, 1tr in each of last 8tr, 1ss in third of first 3ch. (100sts)

Round 10: As Round 5. (120sts)

Round 11: 3ch, 1tr in same place as ss, *1tr in each of next

11tr, 2tr in next tr; rep from * to last 11tr, 1tr in each of last 11tr, 1ss in third of first 3ch. (130sts)

Round 12: 3ch, 1tr in same place as ss, *1tr in each of next 12tr, 2tr in next tr; rep from * to last 12tr, 1tr in each of last 12tr, 1ss in third of first 3ch. (140sts)

Round 13: As Round 7. (160sts)

Round 14: 3ch, 1tr in same place as ss, *1tr in each of next 15tr, 2tr in next tr; rep from * to last 15tr, 1tr in each of last 15tr, 1ss in third of first 3ch. (170sts)

Fasten off.

Sew in ends.

To Make Up

With wrong sides facing each other, join using a double crochet seam (see page 125). Insert the cushion pad halfway round. Finish the double crochet seam with the cushion inside. Fasten off. Puff up cushion into shape.

Edging

The pattern for this stitch works in sections of 8sts. So you need enough stitches to divide equally by eight. To make sure you have 176sts, you will need to increase a total amount of 6sts in next round. Count your stitches at this point and if you have the incorrect amount of stitches, decrease or increase to make sure you have enough to be divided by 8.

Round 1: Using yarn B and hook size 5.00mm, insert hook into first stitch, join yarn with a ss. Make 1inc at beginning of round by making 2dc into next st. *Make 1dc into next 27sts. Make 2dc into next st* Repeat four times, 1dc into each st until end (176sts).

Round 2: *1ch, miss 1st, 1dc 1ch 1htr in next st, miss 1st, 1tr 1ch 1tr in next st, miss 1st, 1htr 1ch 1dc in next st, 1ch, miss 1st, 1ss in next st, rep from * to end placing the last ss in beg of round.

Round 3: *1dc, 1htr in next ch sp, 3tr in next ch sp, 3dtr 1ch 3dtr in next ch sp, 3tr in next ch sp, 1htr 1dc in next ch sp, 1ss on ss, rep from * to end. Fasten off.

Flower motif (make two)

With hook size 5.00mm and leaving a long tail approx 15.5cm (6in), make 6ch, and join with a ss to make a ring.

Round 1:

Using yarn C, work 15dc into ring catching tail into sts, ss into first dc.

Round 2:

3ch tr2tog (see Tip) over next 2dc. 3ch, ss into next dc. Repeat * to * four more times (five petals). Ss into first dc of previous round.

Round 3:

Using hook size 3.25mm, *1ch, 1dc into next st*. Repeat from * to * until end. Ss into first ch. Fasten off.

Repeat to end of Round 1 to make second flower using yarn D and hook size 3.25mm.

Thread a tapestry needle and weave in and out of stitches in centre of small flower, pull gently to close up hole. Sew small flower onto bigger flower to make a double flower. Thread a yarn sewing needle with yarn and sew double flower into centre of cushion. Weave in yarn ends.

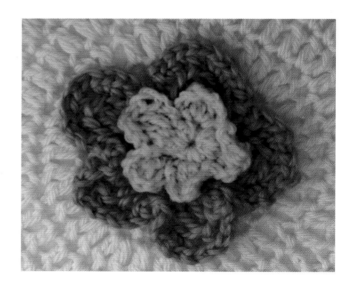

Loopy cushion

Rooster Almerino Aran is the perfect yarn for this cushion; it's made with an equal mix of baby alpaca and merino wool, so it's hard to find anything softer. It is also a beautifully designed cushion, so when displayed in the corner of the sofa or on a comfy chair it will be the envy of everyone who sees it.

MEASUREMENTS
Cushion size 40 x 40cm (15½ x 15½in)

MATERIALS
Rooster Almerino Aran (50g balls)

Yarn A: shade 307, Brighton Rock x 2 balls

Yarn B: shade 308, Spiced Plum x 5 balls

Yarn C: shade 310, Rooster x 2 balls

Yarn D: shade 303, Strawberry Cream x 2 balls

Yarn E: shade 306, Gooseberry x 5 balls

Strip of card measuring 2.1 x 43 cm (¾ x 17in)

4 wooden toggle buttons

Crochet hook size 5.00mm

STITCHES USED
chain stitch, double crochet, loop stitch, slip stitch

ABBREVIATIONS
ch chain	dc double crochet
yrh yarn round hook	ss slip stitch
RS right side	

METHOD
Front piece
Make 61ch using yarn A.

Row 1: Work one row dc.

Row 2 (RS): Work one row dc.

Row 3: (Loop stitch) Insert hook into first st. *pass yarn around piece of card, yrh, draw through two loops, insert hook into next st.* Repeat along row, these loops are formed on the back of the work, pull out strip of card.

Row 4: Work one row dc.

Row 5: Change to yarn B. Work loop st row as Row 3.

Row 6: Work one row dc.

Row 7: Change to yarn C. Work loop st row as Row 3.

Row 8: Work one row dc.

Row 9: Change to yarn D. Work one row dc.

Row 10: Work one row dc.

Row 11: Change to yarn E. Work loop st row as Row 3.

Row 12: Work one row dc.

Row 13: Change to yarn A. Work loop st row as Row 3.

Row 14: Work one row dc.

Row 15: Change to yarn B. Work one row dc.

Row 16: Work one row dc.

Row 17: Change to yarn C. Work loop st row as Row 3.

Row 18: Work one row dc.

Row 19: Change to yarn D. Work loop st row as Row 3.

Row 20: Work one row dc.

Row 21: Change to yarn E. Work one row dc.

Row 22: Work one row dc.

Row 23: Change to yarn A, Work loop st row as Row 3.

Row 24: Work one row dc.

Row 25: Change to yarn E. Work loop st row as Row 3.

Row 26: Work one row dc.

Row 27: Work one row dc.

Row 28: Work one row dc.

Row 29: Work loop st row as Row 3.

Row 30: Work one row dc.

Row 31: Work loop st row as Row 3.

Row 32: Work one row dc.

Repeat Rows 27 through to 32 until work measures 42cm (16½in), fasten off.

Back piece

Make 61ch using yarn E.

Row 1: Work one row dc.

Row 2: Work one row dc.

Continue in dc until work measures 34cm (13½in) all in yarn E. Fasten off.

Back overlapping flap

Make 61ch using yarn A.

Rows 1–4: Using yarn A, work dc.

Rows 5–6: Using yarn B, work dc.

Rows 7–8: Using yarn C, work dc.

Rows 9–10: Using yarn D, work dc.

Rows 11–12: Using yarn E, work dc.

Rows 13–14: Using yarn A, work dc.

Rows 15–16: Using yarn B, work dc.

Rows 17–18: Using yarn C, work dc.

Rows 19–20: Using yarn D, work dc.

Rows 21–22: Using yarn E, work dc.

Rows 23–24: Using yarn A, work dc. Fasten off.

Buttonholes formed using ch st, continue using yarn A. Rejoin yarn 11sts from edge, 7ch, miss 1dc, 1ss into next dc. Fasten off. *miss 8sts and rejoin yarn again. 7ch, miss 1dc, 1ss into next dc, fasten off.* Repeat from * until four buttonhole loops have been formed.
Sew in all yarn ends.

To Make Up

Sew the beginning edges of cushion front and the back overlapping flap together (both made in yarn colour A) using yarn A.

To opposite end of cushion front sew on back piece edge using yarn E.

Now fold the pieces over so the left and right edges of cushion line up. The sides should be sewn up using yarn E. Ensure all colours meet up and pin pieces in place before sewing up. Where back piece and back overlapping flap meet, make sure the stripy overlapping edge is on the front outside edge of cushion and the back piece overlaps on the inside.

When all pieces are sewn together securely insert cushion through opening formed where overlapping flap lays over the back piece. When the cushion is inside, sew on the buttons to match up with the buttonhole loops on flap edge.

Clutch bag with bow

Choosing the colour for this clutch bag can define it either as an elegant and sophisticated accessory, or a bright, fun bag for make-up, jewellery, or any of those other vital items a girl has to carry in her bag.

MATERIALS
(1 x 50g ball of each colour)
Bag 1 (main picture): Debbie Bliss Cotton DK, shade 24, Pink (main colour), shade 25, Plum (bow)
Bag 2: (this page) Rowan Handknit Cotton, shade 320, Buttercup (main colour), shade 319, Mango Fool (stripe and bow)
Snap fastener (popper)

Crochet hook: size 4.00mm

STITCHES USED
chain, double crochet, slip stitch

ABBREVIATIONS

ch chain	ch sp chain space
dc double crochet	dec decrease
ch sp chain space	rep Repeat
RS right side	ss slip stitch
sp space	yrh yarn round hook
WS wrong side	

METHOD
Make 50ch. *Make 1 extra ch, turn, 1 dc into next ch. Make 1dc into each of the remaining 49ch until the end of the row*.
*Repeat from * to * until your square measures 25.5cm (10in).

Shaping the flap
For the next 16 rows dec 1st at the beginning and end of each row. (To decrease: 1ch, insert hook into first dc, yrh and pull through, insert hook into next dc, yrh and pull through, yrh and pull through all the stitches on hook.) Fasten off. Sew in yarn ends.

Lining the bag
After choosing a lining fabric, place your crochet onto it flat and pin into place. Make sure you have an extra 1.5–2cm (½–¾in) around the edge for a hem. Mark the outline and cut the fabric out. After removing from the crochet, fold and pin hem and hand or machine sew down. The lining should be either the same size or slightly smaller than the crochet. With WS together, pin lining onto crochet. Machine or hand sew into place. Fold bag so that the bottom edge meets the row before the flap shaping begins. Pin. Sew down both folded edges of bag leaving the top open for access.

Making the bow
Make 26ch. *Make 1dc into the next st*. Rep from * to * another 25 times. This forms a row. Rep this row 16 times. Fasten off. You should now have a rectangle of crochet. To shape the bow, fold the square in half to locate the centre. Using a leftover end of the same colour yarn, fasten at the top. Make a long running stitch from centre top to centre bottom. Pull end, gathering at centre and fasten off. You should now have a bow shape. Choose a piece of thin coloured ribbon to tie around the centre to cover gathering. Attach at the back. Now stitch the bow on to centre bottom edge of bag flap.

  Patterns… to get you hooked

Placemat and coaster

A strong double knit cotton was used for this placemat and coaster, but any material works well depending on the look you want for your table. Alternative materials you can use are string, raffia or leather – in such cases use the same pattern but change the size of the hook accordingly.

MATERIALS
(50g balls)
Yarn A: Rowan Handknit Cotton DK, shade 252, Black x 2 balls
Yarn B: Debbie Bliss Cotton DK, shade 29, Blue x 2 balls
Yarn C: Rowan Handknit Cotton DK, shade 205, Linen x 2 balls

Crochet hook size: 5.00mm

STITCHES USED
double crochet, slip stitch

ABBREVIATIONS
ch chain   dc double crochet
ss slip stitch   inc increase

METHOD
Placemat
Using yarn A make 4ch. Join with a ss in first ch to form a ring. Work in a spiral as follows marking rounds as you go.

Round 1: Work 8dc into ring.
Round 2: (1dc, inc in next dc) four times. (12sts)
Round 3: (1dc, inc in next dc) six times. (18sts)
Round 4: Change to yarn B, (1dc, inc in next dc) nine times. (27sts)
Round 5: (2dc, inc in next dc) nine times. (36sts)
Round 6: Change to yarn C, 1dc into each dc. (36sts)

Round 7: (3dc, inc in next dc) nine times. (45sts)
Round 8: Change to yarn A, 1dc into each dc. (45sts)
Round 9: Change to yarn C, (4dc, inc in next dc) nine times. (54sts)
Round 10: 1dc into each dc. (54sts)
Round 11: Change to yarn B (5dc, inc in next dc) nine times. (63sts)
Round 12: 1dc into each dc. (63sts)
Round 13: (3dc, inc in next dc, 3dc) nine times. (72sts)
Round 14: Change to yarn A (7dc, inc in next dc) nine times. (81sts)
Round 15: 1ss into each dc, fasten off.

Weave in all yarn ends and steam flat.

Coaster
Using yarn A make 4ch. Join with a ss in first ch to form a ring.

Round 1: Work 8dc into ring.
Round 2: (1dc, inc in next dc) four times. (12sts)
Round 3: Change to yarn B (1dc, inc in next dc) six times. (18sts)
Round 4: (1dc, inc in next dc) nine times. (27sts)
Round 5: Change to yarn C (2dc, inc in next dc) nine times. (36sts)
Round 6: Change to yarn B 1dc into each dc. (36sts)
Round 7: Change to yarn A (3dc, inc in next dc) nine times. (45sts)
Round 8: 1ss into each dc, fasten off.

Weave in ends and steam flat.

Love Questionnaire

1. **What do you wear when you're trying to attract the opposite sex?**
   a. Full evening dress with high heels
   b. Sexy miniskirt and a boob tube
   c. A hip skinny crocheted stripy scarf worn with a denim skirt and big boots

2. **On your first date where would you go?**
   a. To the cinema
   b. To a club
   c. Knit/Crochet club night/Stitch 'n' Bitch group

3. **What tickets would you like to be given for your first date with a new man?**
   a. Green Day gig
   b. Popular West End/Broadway show
   c. As an audience member of a Craft TV network, where you participate in a crochet circle full of men and women who crochet

4. **Where would you go for a weekend away with your partner?**
   a. 5-star hotel with spa
   b Somewhere in the Alps in a log cabin
   c. Visit a sheep farm in northern Scotland where they spin their own fleece from the underbelly of a sheep that eats seaweed in its diet

5. **What's your favourite swimwear your partner wears?**
   a. Surf shorts/bikini
   b. Speedos
   c. Crocheted cotton swimming trunks/bikini in the latest colours

6. **On a date which sporting event would you prefer to be taken to?**
   a. Rugby
   b. Netball
   c. The world's fastest crochet competition

7. **On a cosy night in with your partner would you prefer?**
   a. To snuggle up on the sofa listening to music
   b. Eat a TV dinner and a bag of popcorn
   c. Do a joint crochet project where you crochet each other a beanie hat

8. **What do you look for in a partner?**
   a. Beautiful eyes
   b., Good personality
   c. Strong arms to hold up your hanks of wool, whilst you wind it into a ball

ANSWERS:

Mostly a's:
You take life too seriously. Go straight to your computer, go online and find your nearest Knit/Crochet group and join immediately.

Mostly b's:
You're in danger of letting life pass you by, You'll never find a partner if you continue in this way. You need to crochet more, go and buy a hook and some yarn and make the scarf on page 167.

Mostly c's:
What a wonderful person you are. You must attract potential partners every time you set your crocheted slipper outside the door.

★ Stockists

UK

Bauble (hand-made glass buttons)
32 Brambles Enterprise Centre
Waterberry Drive
Waterlooville
Hampshire PO7 7TH
t: 01243 373706
e: shelley@bauble.uk.com
w: bauble.uk.com

Colinette Yarns Ltd
Banwy Workshops
Llanfair Caereinion
Powys
Wales SY21 0SG
t: 01938 810128
e: info@colinette.com
w: colinette.com

Designer Yarns
Unit 8–10
Newbridge Industrial Estate
Pitt Street
Keighley
W Yorkshire BD21 4PQ
t: 01535 664222
e: jane@designeryarns.uk.com
w: designeryarns.uk.com

Heritage Buttons Ltd
Windmill Park
Halnaker
West Sussex PO18 0NF
t: 01243 77462

HobbyCraft Group Ltd
7 Enterprise Way
Aviation Park
Bournemouth International
Airport
Christchurch
Dorset BH23 6HG
t: 01202 596100
e: customerservices@
hobbycraft.co.uk
w: hobbycraft.co.uk

Injabulo Buttons
Broom Cottage
Ashton
Oundle
Peterborough PE8 5LD
t: 01832 274881
e: info@injabulo.com
w: injabulo.com

Laughing Hens
Southover Nurseries
Spring Lane
Burwash
East Sussex TN19 7JB

t: 01435 884010
e: info@laughinghens.com
w: laughinghens.com

Rooster Yarns
Southover Nurseries
Spring Lane
Burwash
East Sussex TN19 7JB
t: 01435 884010
e: info@roosteryarns.com
w: roosteryarns.com

Rowan Yarns
Green Lane Mill
Holmfirth
HD9 2DX
t: 1484 681881
w: knitrowan.co.uk

Vogue Crochet Hooks
t: 0208 510 9941
e: akgunlu@msn.com
w: diktex.com

USA

Knit Café
8441 Melrose Avenue
Los Angeles
CA 90069
USA

t: 001 323 658 5648
e: knitcafe@aol.com
w: knitcafe.com

The Knitting Garden
25 Long Meadow Road
Uxbridge
MA 01569
USA
t: 001 888 381 9276
e: elizabether@ theknittinggarden.
com
w: theknittinggarden.com

Knitting Fever Inc
35 Debevoise Avenue
Roosevelt
NY 11575
USA
w: knittingfever.com

Purl
137 Sullivan Street
New York
NY 10012
USA
t: 001 212 420 8796
e: customerservice@purlsoho.com
w: store.purlsoho.com

★ Useful addresses

British Hand Knitting Confederation
w: bhkc.co.uk
e: geraldine.bhkc@dsl.pipex.com

Cast Off
w: castoff.info
e: info@castoff.info

Crafts Council (UK)
44a Pentonville Road
London N1 9BY
t: 0044 (0)207 278 7700
w: craftscouncil.org.uk

Knitting & Crochet Guild (UK)
PO Box HH1
Leeds LS8 2YB
w: knitting-and-crochetguild.
org.uk

The Knitting Guild of America
PO Box 3388
Zanesville
OH 43702-3388
USA
w: tkga.com
e: tkga@tkga.com

WEBSITES

There are a feast of amazing and interesting crochet websites. The following websites were relevant at the time of press. If they are no longer there, just type the word 'crochet' into a search engine and all sorts of interesting sites appear and lure you into the world of crochet.

Crochet Couture: anacam.com/hats
Crochet for men: crochetformen.blogmatrix.com
Crochet Sculpture: mysung.tripod.com/artscape.html
Knitting Magazine: knitty.com
Not Your Granny's   crochet.nearlythere.com/cgi-bin/
Crochet: wiki.cgi/Not_Your_Granny's_Crochet

Index

abbreviations
crochet 139
knitting 37, 55
acrylic yarn 13, 14, 23, 46
Afghan blankets 101
Afghan crochet 103
alpaca 23, 62, 107
angora 23
Aran (worsted) yarn 23, 109
art forms 103–104

back stitch seam 44, 125
bags
beaded make-up bag 54,
    82–83
beaded purse 138, 172–173
button handbag 54, 86
clutch bag with bow 184–185
mesh bag 138, 154–156
yarn tote bag 53, 94–95
bamboo needles 25
beading 48
    beaded make-up bag 54,
        82–83
beaded purse 138, 172–173
crochet beading 124
flower-power beaded belt 137,
    162–163
threading beads 48
beanie hats 81, 137, 140–141
belt, beaded 137, 162–163
bikini 54, 72–73
blankets
Afghan blankets 101
flower blanket 137, 142–143
stripy dog blanket 138, 150–
    151
blocking 46, 135

borders, picking up stitches for
    42
bows 51
clutch bag with bow 184–185
buttonholes 42
buttons 27, 111
button handbag 54, 86
Pierrot button 131
two-color button 131

cable needles 25
camisole 148–149
cardigans
Alpaca cardigan 62–65
tie bolero 137, 157–161
carrying and storing
crochet 133
knitting 28
cashmere 23
Cast Off 16
casting off (binding off) 34
casting on 30
slip knots 30
two-needle method 30
celebrity knitters and
crocheters 15, 102
cell phone/iPod cover 53, 54,
    74–75
chain 114
chain space, working into 117
turning chains 119
charity stores 21, 132
chunky yarns 23, 109
circular needles 25
clusters 117
clutch bag with bow 184–185
colors, changing 35, 38
cotton yarn 23, 107

crochet 100–189
Afghan crochet 103
carrying and storing 133
decorations 128–131
edgings 126–127
equipment 110–111
filet crochet 103
freeform crochet 104
patterns 123, 136–187
simple crochet 103
stitches 114–118
techniques 113, 119–127
washing, blocking and
steaming 134–135
yarns 101, 103, 107, 109, 132,
    137
crochet quiz 105
cushions
cushion cake 137, 178–180
funky cushions 84–85
loopy cushion 137, 181–183

damp finishing 45–46, 135
dating tips for knitters 18
decorations 48–51, 128–131
department stores 21, 132
dog blanket 138, 150–151
dog jackets 53, 87–89
pom-pom coat 87, 89
shark coat 87, 88–89
double crochet 116
double crochet cluster 117
double knitting yarn 23, 109
double-pointed needles 25
dropped stitches 40
dry cleaning 47

eBay 21

edgings 126–127
equipment
crochet 110–111
knitting 24–27
eyelash yarn 23, 80, 107

Fairisle patterns 38–39
fancy yarns 109
fashion design 7, 102
fastening off/finishing 122
filet crochet 103
fingering weight yarn 109
finishing a project 45–47
blocking 46, 135
damp finishing 45–46, 135
pressing 46–47
washing 47, 134
fishermens' sweaters 11
flowers 51, 131
flower blanket 137, 142–143
flower-power beaded belt 137,
    162–163
summer flower camisole 148–
    149
4 ply yarn 23, 109
freeform crochet 104
frill edging 127
frill shawl 137, 144–145
fringes 50, 130
fur, fake 53, 96

garter stitch 32, 78
gauge 112
gauge square 112
gloves, fingerless 66–67, 137,
    170–171
guerilla knitters 16

hairbands, striped 152–153

hairy yarns see eyelash yarn

half double crochet 116

hanks and skeins 24

hats

beanie hats 81, 137, 140–141

cotton summer hat 70–71

summer brimmed hat 137, 164–166

history of knitting 11–13

hoody 58–61

hooks 27, 110

holding 113

size conversion chart 110

storing 133

hosiery 11

hot-water bottle cover 137, 176–177

increasing and decreasing (crochet) 121–122

increasing and decreasing (knitting) 33

intarsia technique 54, 73

internet 16, 21, 132

ironing 134

joining yarns 35, 121

Karan, Donna 7

knit stitch 31

knitting 10–99

carrying and storing 28

decorations 48–51

equipment 24–27

mistakes 98

patterns 36–39, 52–97

problem-solving 40–41

stitches 31–32

techniques 29–39

yarns 14, 21–24

knitting and crochet groups 8, 9, 16, 17, 19, 101–102

labels, yarn 24, 110

leather strips 109

leg warmers 76

lining work 184

love questionnaire 188

McCartney, Stella 7

machine-knitted items 12

McQueen, Alexander 7

make-up bag 54, 82–83

male knitters and crocheters 8, 17, 102

mattress stitch 45

merino wool 21

mesh bag 138, 154–156

mohair 23

moss stitch 62

moths 28

needle case 53, 96–97

needle protectors 27

needles 24–25

bamboo needles 25

cable needles 25

circular needles 25

double-pointed needles 25

holding 29

measurements 24

supersize needles 14, 23

width 24–25

number of knitters (US) 16

over-and-under knitting 38

patterns

crochet 123, 136–187

knitting 36–39, 52–97

sizing 36

US/UK terminology 123

pets

dog jackets 53, 87–89

playmat 138, 146–147

stripy dog blanket 138, 150–151

picot edging 126

pins 27, 111

placemat and coaster 186–187

ply 23, 109

Aran (worsted) 23, 109

chunky 23, 109

double knitting (DK) 23, 109

4 ply 23, 109

superchunky 14, 23, 109

pom-poms 49, 129

daisy cashmere scarf 167–169

hot-water bottle cover 137, 176–177

mini pom-poms 129

pom-pom dog coat 87, 89

poncho 68–69

popcorn (crochet stitch) 118

popularity of knitting and crochet 7–9, 14–15, 101–102

pressing 46–47

purl stitch 31

raffia 109

rags 109

ribbing 33

ribbon yarn 23, 107

ribbons

Alpaca cardigan 62–65

ribbon slippers 137, 174–175

rose tank top 90–93

right and wrong sides of your work 32

rounds, working in the 25, 120

row counters 27

Rowan Yarns 101

rows

losing your place 41

unravelling 41

working in 119

runs 40

scarves

daisy cashmere scarf 137, 167–169

fluffy silky-chic scarf 80

garter stitch scarf 78–79

tassled scarf 53, 78–79

scissors 25, 111

seams

back stitch 44, 125

crochet 124–125

joining two cast-off edges 45

knitting 44–45

mattress stitch 45

over-and-over method 44

single crochet seam 125

slip stitch seam 125

woven seam 125

sewing in ends 43

sewing up/making up 37, 43

sewing-up needle 27

shawl, frilled 137, 144–145

shell edging 126

silk yarn 23, 107

single crochet 115
single crochet edging 126
single crochet seam 125
sizing (patterns) 36
slip knot 30
slip stitch 115
slip stitch seam 125
slippers 137, 174–175
sport weight yarn 109
squares, making 121
steaming 46
stitch holders 27
Stitch 'n' Bitch 16, 102
stitch problems
dropped stitches 40
runs 40
twisted stitches 40
undoing stitches 41
stitches (crochet)
chain 114
double crochet 116
double crochet cluster 117
half double crochet 116
popcorn 118
single crochet 115
slip loop 114
slip stitch 115
treble 117
working into a chain space 117
stitches (knitting)
back stitch 44
garter stitch 32, 78
knit stitch 31
mattress stitch 45
moss stitch 62
picking up stitches 42
purl stitch 31

stockinette stitch 32
stockinette stitch 32
string/twine 103, 109
superchunky yarns 14, 23, 109
supersize needles 14, 23
suppliers 99, 189
sweaters
easy sweater 54, 56–57
rose tank top 90–93
unisex hoody 58–61

tank top 90–93
tape measure 25, 111
tassels 50, 130
tassled scarf 53, 79
techniques (crochet) 119–127
beading 124
edgings 126–127
fastening off/finishing 122
increasing and decreasing 121–122
joining yarns 121
rounds, working in 120
seams 124–125
squares, making 121
turning the work 119
weaving/sewing in ends 122
working in rows 119
see also stitches
techniques (knitting) 29–39
buttonholes 42
casting off (binding off) 34
casting on 30
holding the needles 29
holding the yarn 29
increasing and decreasing 33
joining yarn 35
knitting a stitch 31

picking up stitches for borders 42
purling a stitch 31
ribbing 33
right and wrong sides of your work 32
sewing in ends 43
sewing seams 44–45
sewing up/making up 43
slipping a stitch 32
tension squares 34
washing, blocking and steaming 45–47
see also stitches
tension 29
tension squares 34
therapeutic benefits 9, 15, 17
throw 77
tie bolero 157–161
treble 117
turning the work 119
twisted stitches 40
twisting method (colored yarn) 38

washing
crochet 134
dry cleaning 47
hand-washing 47, 134
knitting 47
machine washing 47, 134
weaving/sewing in ends 122
wool sewing needles 111
wool yarns 14, 21, 23, 107
woven seam 125

yarn
acrylic 13, 14, 23, 46

alpaca 23, 62, 107
angora 23
buying 21, 132
cashmere 23
cotton 23, 107
crochet 107, 109
crochet yarns 101, 103, 107, 132, 137
eyelash yarn 23, 80, 107
fancy yarns 109
hanks and skeins 24
holding the yarn (crochet) 113
holding the yarn (knitting) 29
joining yarn (crochet) 121
joining yarn (knitting) 35
knitting yarns 14, 21–24
labels 24, 110
leather strips 109
mohair 23
quantities 36
raffia 109
rags 109
ribbon yarn 23, 107
silk 23, 107
storing 133
string/twine 103, 109
weights and lengths 24
wool 14, 21, 23, 107
see also ply
yarn tote bag 53, 94–95 C: